Grammar Sense 2A

SERIES DIRECTOR
Susan Kesner Bland

Cheryl Pavlik

OXFORD
UNIVERSITY PRESS

UNIVERSITY PRESS

198 Madison Avenue
New York, NY 10016 USA

Great Clarendon Street, Oxford OX2 6DP UK

Oxford University Press is a department of the University of Oxford.
It furthers the University's objective of excellence in research, scholarship,
and education by publishing worldwide in

Oxford New York

Auckland Cape Town Dar es Salaam Hong Kong Karachi
Kuala Lumpur Madrid Melbourne Mexico City Nairobi
New Delhi Shanghai Taipei Toronto

With offices in

Argentina Austria Brazil Chile Czech Republic France Greece
Guatemala Hungary Italy Japan Poland Portugal Singapore
South Korea Switzerland Thailand Turkey Ukraine Vietnam

OXFORD and OXFORD ENGLISH are registered trademarks of
Oxford University Press

Editorial Manager: Janet Aitchison
Senior Editor: Stephanie Karras
Editor: Diane Flanel Piniaris
Associate Editor: Kim Steiner
Art Director: Lynn Luchetti
Design Project Manager: Mary Chandler
Designer (cover): Lee Anne Dollison
Senior Art Editor: Jodi Waxman
Art Editor: Judi DeSouter
Production Manager: Shanta Persaud
Production Controller: Eve Wong

ISBN: 978 019 436572 7

Printed in Hong Kong.

10 9 8 7 6 5 4 3

Book design: Bill Smith Studio
Composition: Compset, Inc.
Indexer: Leonard Neufeld

ACKNOWLEDGMENTS

Cover image: © Kevin Schafer / Peter Arnold, Inc.

Illustrations by:
Barbara Bastian, Lyndall Culbertson, Mike Hortens Design,
Patrick Faricy, Paul Hampson, Randy Jones, Jon Keegan,
Laura Hartman Maestro, Tom Newsom, Roger Penwill,
Alan Reingold, Don Stewart, Bill Thomson, Scott Tysick /
Masterfile, Bob Wilson

*The publisher would like to thank the following for their permission
to reproduce photographs:*
Macduff Everton / CORBIS; Tom Brakefield / Bruce
Coleman, Inc.; Wally McNamee / CORBIS; Ron Russell /
ImageState; photograph of Voyager: NASA, JPL, and
Caltech; Associated Press; Hulton Archive / Getty Images;
Ted Streshinsky / CORBIS; Rosenberg Library, Galveston,
Texas; Keith Black / Index Stock Imagery; PhotoDisc;
Comstock; Robin Lynne Gibson / Getty Images; Eric Futran
/ FoodPix; Bettmann / CORBIS; Patrick Robert / Corbis
Sygma; W. Bibikow / Jonarnold.com; Eye-Wire / Getty
Images; Rob Gage / Getty Images; Ken Reid / Getty Images;
Renee Lynn / Photo Researchers, Inc.; Ron Cohn / The
Gorilla Foundation; Dan Suzio / Photo Researchers, Inc.;
Will and Deni Mcintyre / Getty Images / Stone;
Hammecher Schlemmer; Jodi Waxman / OUP; Roy Morsch
/ CORBIS; PhotoAlto / Robert Harding World Imagery;
Pictures Colour Library; Duomo / CORBIS

*The publisher would like to thank the following for their permission
to reproduce these extracts and adaptations of copyrighted
material:*
pp. 4-5. "Mysterious Island." This article first appeared in
The Christian Science Monitor on June 16, 1998, and is
reproduced with permission. © 1998 The Christian Science
Publishing Society. All rights reserved; **pp. 48-49.** "The
Decade That Mattered." ©1991 Time Inc. Reprinted by
ermission; pp. 90–91. "This man's been nearly everywhere."
This article first appeared in *The Christian Science Monitor* on
March 10, 1998, and is reproduced with permission. ©
1998 The Christian Science Publishing Society. All rights
reserved.

Acknowledgements

It takes a village to write a grammar series. I am humbled by the expertise of all those who have contributed in so many ways.

I am grateful to Cheryl Pavlik for her intellectual curiosity, creativity, wit, and for her friendship. A special thanks goes to Stephanie Karras for putting all of the pieces together with such commitment and superb organizational and problem-solving skills, mixed with just the right amount of levity. I owe a special debt of gratitude to Janet Aitchison for her continued support and encouragement from the very beginning, and for her help with the big issues as well as the small details.

It has been a pleasure working closely with Diane Flanel Piniaris, Pietro Alongi, Andrew Gitzy, James Morgan, Nan Clarke, Randee Falk, and Marietta Urban. Their comments, questions, grammar insights, and creative solutions have been invaluable. Many thanks also go to the talented editorial, production, and design staff at Oxford University Press; to Susan Lanzano for her role in getting this project started; and to Susan Mraz for her help in the early stages.

Finally, I owe everything to my family, Bob, Jenny, and Scott, for always being there for me, as well as for their amusing views about everything, especially grammar.

Susan Kesner Bland,
Series Director

The Series Director and Publisher would like to acknowledge the following individuals for their invaluable input during the development of this series:

Harriet Allison, Atlanta College of Art, GA; **Alex Baez,** Southwest Texas State University, TX; **Nathalie Bailey,** Lehman College, CUNY, NY; **Jamie Beaton,** Boston University, MA; **Michael Berman,** Montgomery College, MD; **Angela Blackwell,** San Francisco State University, CA; **Vera Bradford,** IBEU, Rio de Janerio, Brazil; **Glenda Bro,** Mount San Antonio Community College, CA; **Jennifer Burton,** University of California, San Francisco, CA; **Magali Duignan,** Augusta State University, GA; **Anne Ediger,** Hunter College, CUNY, NY; **Joyce Grabowski,** Flushing High School, NY; **Virginia Heringer,** Pasadena City College, CA; **Rocia Hernandez,** Mexico City, Mexico; **Nancy Herzfeld-Pipkin,** University of California, San Diego, CA; **Michelle Johnstone,** Mexico City, Mexico; **Kate de Jong,** University of California, San Diego, CA; **Pamela Kennedy,** Holyoke Community College, MA; **Jean McConochie,** Pace University, NY; **Karen McRobie,** Golden Gate University, CA; **Elizabeth Neblett,** Union County College, NJ; **Dian Perkins,** Wheeling High School, IL; **Fausto Rocha de Marcos Rebelo,** Recife, Brazil; **Mildred Rugger,** Southwest Texas State University, TX; **Dawn Schmidt,** California State University, San Marcos, CA; **Katharine Sherak,** San Francisco State University, CA; **Lois Spitzer,** University of Nebraska-Lincoln, NE; **Laura Stering,** University of California, San Francisco, CA; **Annie Stumpfhauser,** Morelios, Mexico; **Anthea Tillyer,** Hunter College, CUNY, NY; **Julie Un,** Massasoit Community College, MA; **Susan Walker,** SUNY New Paltz, NY; **Cheryl Wecksler,** California State University, San Marcos, CA; **Teresa Wise,** Georgia State University, GA.

Contents

PART 3: The Future

PART 4: Modals

Introduction

Grammar Sense: A Discourse-Based Approach

Grammar Sense is a comprehensive four-level grammar series based on the authentic use of English grammar in discourse. The grammar is systematically organized, explained, and practiced in a communicative, learner-centered environment, making it easily teachable and learnable.

Many people ask, why learn grammar? The answer is simple: meaningful communication depends on our ability to connect form and meaning appropriately. In order to do so, we must consider such factors as intention, attitude, and social relationships, in addition to the contexts of time and place. All of these factors make up a discourse setting. For example, we use the present continuous not only to describe an activity in progress *(He's working.)*, but also to complain *(He's always working.)*, to describe a planned event in the future *(He's working tomorrow.)*, and to describe temporary or unusual behavior *(He's being lazy at work.)*. It is only through examination of the discourse setting that the different meanings and uses of the present continuous can be distinguished from one another. A discourse-based approach provides students with the tools for making sense of the grammar of natural language by systematically explaining *who, what, where, when, why,* and *how* for each grammatical form.

Systematically Organized Syllabus

Learning grammar is a developmental process that occurs gradually. In *Grammar Sense* the careful sequencing, systematic repetition, recycling, review, and expansion promote grammatical awareness and fluency.

Level 1 (basic level) focuses on building an elementary understanding of form, meaning, and use as students develop basic oral language skills in short conversations and discussions. Level 1 also targets the grammar skills involved in writing short paragraphs, using basic cohesive devices such as conjunctions and pronouns.

At **Level 2 (intermediate level)** the focus turns to expanding the basic understanding of form, meaning, and use in longer and more varied discourse settings, and with more complex grammatical structures and academic themes. Level 2 emphasizes grammar skills beyond the sentence level, as students begin to initiate and sustain conversations and discussions, and progress toward longer types of writing.

At **Level 3 (high intermediate)** the focus moves to spoken and written grammar in academic discourse settings, often in contexts that are conceptually more challenging and abstract. Level 3 emphasizes consistent and appropriate language use, especially of those aspects of grammar needed in extended conversations and discussions, and in longer academic and personal writing.

Finally, at **Level 4** (**advanced**) the focus shifts to written grammar for the purpose of academic writing. There is increased emphasis on meaning and use and on self-editing skills, on the assumption that advanced level students have mastered much of the basic structure of the language, but still need help in transferring this knowledge to more effective, concise, and grammatically correct academic writing.

Introduction of Form Before Meaning and Use

Form is introduced and practiced in a separate section before meaning and use. This ensures that students understand what the form looks like and sounds like at the sentence level, before engaging in more challenging and open-ended activities that concentrate on meaning and use.

Focus on Natural Language Use

Grammar Sense uses authentic reading texts and examples that are based on or quoted verbatim from actual English-language sources to provide a true picture of natural language use. To avoid unnatural language, the themes of the introductory reading texts are only subtly touched upon throughout a chapter. The focus thus remains on typical examples of the most common meanings and uses.

Exposure to authentic language helps students bridge the gap between the classroom and the outside world by encouraging awareness of the "grammar" all around them in daily life: in magazines, newspapers, package instructions, television shows, signs, and so on. Becoming language-aware is an important step in the language-learning process: Students generalize from the examples they find and apply their understanding to their independent language use in daily living, at work, or as they further their education.

Special Sections to Extend Grammatical Knowledge

Understanding grammar as a system entails understanding how different parts of the language support and interact with the target structure. *Grammar Sense* features special sections at strategic points throughout the text to highlight relevant lexical and discourse issues.

- **Beyond the Sentence** sections focus on the structure as it is used in extended discourse to help improve students' writing skills. These sections highlight such issues as how grammatical forms are used to avoid redundancy, and how to change or maintain focus.

- **Informally Speaking** sections highlight the differences between written and spoken language. This understanding is crucial for achieving second language fluency. Reduced forms, omissions, and pronunciation changes are explained in order to improve aural comprehension.

- **Pronunciation Notes** show students how to pronounce selected forms of the target language, such as the regular simple past ending -*ed*.

- **Vocabulary Notes** provide succinct presentations of words and phrases that are commonly used with the target structure, such as time expressions associated with the simple present and simple past.simple present and simple past.

Student-Centered Presentation and Practice

Student-centered presentation and practice allow learners at all levels to discover the grammar in pairs, groups, and individually, in both the Form and in the Meaning and Use sections of each chapter. Numerous inductive activities encourage students to use their problem-solving abilities to gain the skills, experience, and confidence to use English outside of class and to continue learning on their own.

Flexibility to Suit Any Classroom Situation

Grammar Sense offers teachers great flexibility with hundreds of intellectually engaging exercises to choose from. Teachers may choose to skip chapters or sections within chapters, or teach them in a different order, depending on student needs and time constraints. Each Student Book is self-contained so teachers may choose to use only one book, or the full series, if they wish.

Components at Each Level

- The **Student Book** is intended for classroom use and offers concise charts, level-appropriate explanations, and thorough four-skills practice exercises. Each Student Book is also a useful reference resource with extensive Appendices, a helpful Glossary of Grammar Terms, and a detailed Index.

- The **Audio Cassettes and CDs** feature listening exercises that provide practice discriminating form, understanding meaning and use, and interpreting non-standard forms.

- The **Workbook** has a wealth of additional exercises to supplement those in the Student Book. It is ideal for homework, independent practice, or review. The Answer Key, on easily removable perforated pages, is provided at the back of the book.

- The **Teacher's Book** has many practical ideas and techniques for presenting the Form and the Meaning and Use sections. It also includes troubleshooting advice, cultural notes, and suggestions for additional activities. The Answer Key for the Student Book and the complete Tapescript are also provided.

- The **ExamView® Assessment CD-ROM** allows you to create fully-customized tests and provides the option to add your own test items. It offers thousands of different evaluation exercises correlated to each level of *Grammar Sense*.

- **TOEFL®-Style Tests** and Answer Keys, along with advice on conducting the tests and interpreting the results, are available for teachers to download from the Internet. (See *Grammar Sense Teacher's Book 2* for the website address.)

Tour of a Chapter

Each chapter in *Grammar Sense* follows this format:

The **Grammar in Discourse** section introduces the target structure in its natural context via a high-interest authentic reading text.

> • *Authentic reading texts show how language is really used.*

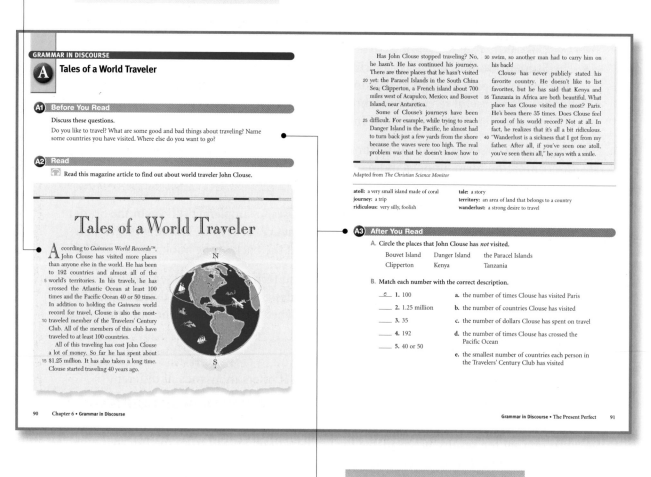

GRAMMAR IN DISCOURSE

A Tales of a World Traveler

A1 Before You Read

Discuss these questions.

Do you like to travel? What are some good and bad things about traveling? Name some countries you have visited. Where else do you want to go?

A2 Read

Read this magazine article to find out about world traveler John Clouse.

Tales of a World Traveler

According to *Guinness World Records*™, John Clouse has visited more places than anyone else in the world. He has been to 192 countries and almost all of the
5 world's territories. In his travels, he has crossed the Atlantic Ocean at least 100 times and the Pacific Ocean 40 or 50 times. In addition to holding the *Guinness* world record for travel, Clouse is also the most-
10 traveled member of the Travelers' Century Club. All of the members of this club have traveled to at least 100 countries.

All of this traveling has cost John Clouse a lot of money. So far he has spent about
15 $1.25 million. It has also taken a long time. Clouse started traveling 40 years ago.

Has John Clouse stopped traveling? No, he hasn't. He has continued his journeys. There are three places that he hasn't visited
20 yet: the Paracel Islands in the South China Sea; Clipperton, a French island about 700 miles west of Acapulco, Mexico; and Bouvet Island, near Antarctica.

Some of Clouse's journeys have been
25 difficult. For example, while trying to reach Danger Island in the Pacific, he almost had to turn back just a few yards from the shore because the waves were too high. The real problem was that he doesn't know how to
30 swim, so another man had to carry him on his back!

Clouse has never publicly stated his favorite country. He doesn't like to list favorites, but he has said that Kenya and
35 Tanzania in Africa are both beautiful. What place has Clouse visited the most? Paris. He's been there 35 times. Does Clouse feel proud of his world record? Not at all. In fact, he realizes that it's all a bit ridiculous.
40 "Wanderlust is a sickness that I got from my father. After all, if you've seen one atoll, you've seen them all," he says with a smile.

Adapted from *The Christian Science Monitor*

atoll: a very small island made of coral
journey: a trip
ridiculous: very silly, foolish
tale: a story
territory: an area of land that belongs to a country
wanderlust: a strong desire to travel

A3 After You Read

A. Circle the places that John Clouse has *not* visited.

Bouvet Island   Danger Island   the Paracel Islands
Clipperton   Kenya   Tanzania

B. Match each number with the correct description.

_e_ 1. 100   a. the number of times Clouse has visited Paris
____ 2. 1.25 million   b. the number of countries Clouse has visited
____ 3. 35   c. the number of dollars Clouse has spent on travel
____ 4. 192   d. the number of times Clouse has crossed the Pacific Ocean
____ 5. 40 or 50   e. the smallest number of countries each person in the Travelers' Century Club has visited

90   Chapter 6 • Grammar in Discourse

Grammar in Discourse • The Present Perfect   91

> • *Structured reading tasks help students read and understand the text.*

The **Form** section(s) provides clear presentation of the target structure, detailed notes, and thorough practice exercises.

• Inductive **Examining Form** exercises encourage students to think about how to form the target structure.

B The Present Perfect

Examining Form

Look at the sentences and complete the tasks below. Then discuss your answers and read the Form charts to check them.

1a. He has crossed the Atlantic many times.
1b. He crossed the Atlantic in 1999.
2a. They flew to Paris last night.
2b. They have flown to Paris many times.

1. Which two sentences are in the simple past? Which two sentences are in the present perfect? How many words are necessary to form the present perfect?

2. Underline the verb forms that follow *has* and *have*. These are past participles. Which form resembles the simple past? Which form is irregular?

3. Look back at the article on page 90. Find five examples of the present perfect.

Affirmative Statements

SUBJECT	HAVE/HAS	PAST PARTICIPLE	
I	have		
You			
He			
She	has	traveled flown	to Paris.
It			
We			
You	have		
They			

CONTRACTIONS		
I've		
She's	traveled	to Paris.
They've		

Negative Statements

SUBJECT	HAVE/HAS	NOT	PAST PARTICIPLE	
I	have			
You				
He				
She	has	not	traveled flown	to Paris.
It				
We				
You	have			
They				

CONTRACTIONS		
I	haven't	
She	hasn't	traveled	to Paris.
They	haven't	

Yes/No Questions

HAVE/HAS	SUBJECT	PAST PARTICIPLE	
Have	you		
Has	it	traveled flown	to Paris?
Have	they		

Short Answers

YES	SUBJECT	HAVE/HAS		NO	SUBJECT	HAVE/HAS + NOT
	I	have.			I	haven't.
Yes,	he	has.		No,	he	hasn't.
	they	have.			they	haven't.

Information Questions

WH- WORD	HAVE/HAS	SUBJECT	PAST PARTICIPLE	
Who	have	you	seen?	
What				
Why	has	she	been	in the hospital?
How long	have	they		

WH- WORD (SUBJECT)	HAS		PAST PARTICIPLE	
Who	has		traveled	to Paris?
What			happened?	

• The past participle of a regular verb has the same form as the simple past (verb + -d/-ed). See Appendices 4 and 5 for the spelling and pronunciation of verbs ending in -ed.
• Irregular verbs have special past participle forms. See Appendix 6 for a list of irregular verbs and their past participles.

B4 Completing Conversations with the Present Perfect

A. Complete these conversations with the words in parentheses and the present perfect. Use contractions where possible.

Conversation 1

Silvio: How long _____have_____ you _____lived_____ (live) here?
                 1   2

Victor: Five years. _____ you _____ (be) here long?
                   3   4

Silvio: No, I _____ (not). I _____ only
               5   6

_____ (be) here for six months.
   7

Conversation 2

Gina: Hi, Julie. I _____ (not/see) you for a long time.
            1

Julie: Hi, Gina. I think it _____ (be) almost three years since we last
              2

met. How _____ your family _____ (be)?
     3   4

Gina: Oh, there _____ (be) a lot of changes. My older brother, Chris,
            5

_____ (get) married, and Tony and his wife, Marta,
   6

_____ (have) two children.
   7

B. Practice the conversations in part A with a partner.

B5 Building Sentences

A. Build eight logical sentences: four in the present perfect and four in the simple past. Punctuate your sentences correctly.

Present Perfect: *She has been a good friend.*   Simple Past: *She went to a restaurant.*

		been	for a long time
she	have	waited	to a restaurant
they	has	learned	a good friend
		went	English

B. Rewrite your sentences as negative statements.

• Clear and detailed **Form Charts** make learning the grammar easy.

• A wealth of exercises provide practice in manipulating the form.

The **Meaning and Use** section(s) offers clear and comprehensive explanations of how the target structure is used, and exercises to practice using it appropriately.

• *Inductive **Examining Meaning and Use** exercises encourage students to analyze how we use the target structure.*

MEANING AND USE 1

C Continuing Time Up to Now

C1 Listening for Meaning and Use ► Note 1

Listen to each sentence. Is the speaker talking about a past situation that continues to the present, or a situation that began and ended in the past? Check (✓) the correct column.

MEANING AND USE 2

D Indefinite Past Time

Examining Meaning and Use

Read the sentences and answer the questions below. Then discuss your answers and read the Meaning and Use Notes to check them.

1a. I've flown in an airplane.
1b. I flew to Rome last month.

2a. There have been many car accidents on this road.
2b. There was an accident here yesterday.

1. Which sentences talk about an indefinite (not exact) time in the past? Which form of the verb is used in these sentences?

2. Which sentences mention a definite (exact) time in the past? Which form of the verb is used in these sentences?

Meaning and Use Notes

> **Indefinite Past Time**
>
> **1A** Use the present perfect to talk about actions or states that happened at an indefinite (not exact) time in the past.
>
> A: Have you met Bob?
> B: Yes, I**'ve met** him. He's really nice.
>
> **1B** Actions or states in the present perfect can happen once or repeatedly.
>
> He**'s visited** Hawaii once.
> I**'ve tried** three times to pass my driver's license exam.
>
> **1C** Do not use the present perfect with time expressions that express a definite (exact) time in the past. When you mention the definite time an event happened, use the simple past.
>
> I **went** to Europe in 1999.
> *I've gone to Europe in 1999. (INCORRECT)

100   Chapter 6 • Meaning and Use 2

> **Using *Ever* with Indefinite Past Time**
>
> **2** The adverb *ever* means "at any time." Use *ever* in present perfect questions to ask if an action took place at any time in the past.
>
> A: **Have** you **ever seen** a ghost?
> B: Yes, I have. OR
>   No, I haven't.
>
> ⚠ We usually do not use *ever* in present perfect affirmative statements.
> I **have seen** a ghost.
> * I have ever seen a ghost. (INCORRECT)

D1 Listening for Meaning and Use ► Notes 1A, 1C

Listen to each sentence. Does it refer to a definite time in the past or an indefinite time in the past? Check (✓) the correct column.

	DEFINITE TIME IN THE PAST	INDEFINITE TIME IN THE PAST
1.		✓

D3 Asking Questions About Indefinite Past Time ► Notes 1A, 2

Write two *Yes/No* questions for each of these situations. Use the present perfect.

1. Your friends have traveled a lot. You want to find out about their trips.
Have you ever been to Egypt? Have you seen the pyramids?

2. You are thinking about buying a used car. You meet a woman who is trying to sell her car.

3. You want to hire a babysitter. You are interviewing a teenager for the job.

4. You are looking for a new roommate. Someone comes to see your apartment.

5. Your friend, Lee, has moved to a new town. You want to find out about his experiences.

D4 Describing Progress ► Notes 1A, 1B

Paul has made a list of things to do before he moves to his new apartment. Look at the list and make statements about his progress so far.

He's called the moving company.
He hasn't vacuumed the apartment.

TO DO
✓ Call the moving company
  Vacuum apartment
✓ Disconnect telephone
  Pack all clothes
  Throw away trash
  Contact the post office
✓ Call mom and give her new address
  Clean oven
  Leave key with superintendent

Meaning and Use 2 • The Present Perfect   103

• *Succinct explanations and authentic examples illustrate the various meanings and uses of the structure.*

• *Practice exercises enable students to use the structure appropriately and fluently.*

The **Review** section allows students to demonstrate their mastery of all aspects of the structure. It can be used for further practice or as a test.

• ***Thinking About Meaning and Use** exercises consolidate students' understanding of all aspects of the structure.*

• ***Editing** exercises teach students to correct their own writing.*

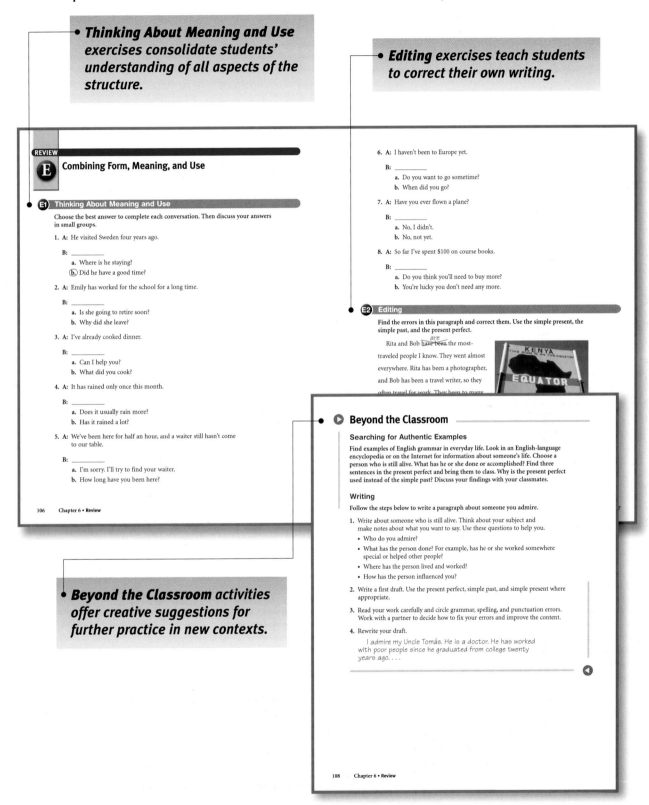

E Combining Form, Meaning, and Use

E1 Thinking About Meaning and Use

Choose the best answer to complete each conversation. Then discuss your answers in small groups.

1. **A:** He visited Sweden four years ago.

   B: _____
   a. Where is he staying?
   b. Did he have a good time?

2. **A:** Emily has worked for the school for a long time.

   B: _____
   a. Is she going to retire soon?
   b. Why did she leave?

3. **A:** I've already cooked dinner.

   B: _____
   a. Can I help you?
   b. What did you cook?

4. **A:** It has rained only once this month.

   B: _____
   a. Does it usually rain more?
   b. Has it rained a lot?

5. **A:** We've been here for half an hour, and a waiter still hasn't come to our table.

   B: _____
   a. I'm sorry. I'll try to find your waiter.
   b. How long have you been here?

6. **A:** I haven't been to Europe yet.

   B: _____
   a. Do you want to go sometime?
   b. When did you go?

7. **A:** Have you ever flown a plane?

   B: _____
   a. No, I didn't.
   b. No, not yet.

8. **A:** So far I've spent $100 on course books.

   B: _____
   a. Do you think you'll need to buy more?
   b. You're lucky you don't need any more.

E2 Editing

Find the errors in this paragraph and correct them. Use the simple present, the simple past, and the present perfect.

Rita and Bob ~~have been~~ *are* the most-traveled people I know. They went almost everywhere. Rita has been a photographer, and Bob has been a travel writer, so they often travel for work. They been to many

• ***Beyond the Classroom** activities offer creative suggestions for further practice in new contexts.*

▶ **Beyond the Classroom**

Searching for Authentic Examples

Find examples of English grammar in everyday life. Look in an English-language encyclopedia or on the Internet for information about someone's life. Choose a person who is still alive. What has he or she done or accomplished? Find three sentences in the present perfect and bring them to class. Why is the present perfect used instead of the simple past? Discuss your findings with your classmates.

Writing

Follow the steps below to write a paragraph about someone you admire.

1. Write about someone who is still alive. Think about your subject and make notes about what you want to say. Use these questions to help you.
   • Who do you admire?
   • What has the person done? For example, has he or she worked somewhere special or helped other people?
   • Where has the person lived and worked?
   • How has the person influenced you?

2. Write a first draft. Use the present perfect, simple past, and simple present where appropriate.

3. Read your work carefully and circle grammar, spelling, and punctuation errors. Work with a partner to decide how to fix your errors and improve the content.

4. Rewrite your draft.

   I admire my Uncle Tomás. He is a doctor. He has worked with poor people since he graduated from college twenty years ago. . . .

◀

Special Sections appear throughout the chapters, with clear explanations, authentic examples, and follow-up exercises.

*• **Pronunciation Notes** show students how to pronounce selected forms of the target language.*

*• **Beyond the Sentence** sections show how structures function differently in extended discourse.*

Pronunciation Notes

Pronunciation of Verbs Ending in -ed

The regular simple past ending -ed is pronounced in three different ways, depending on the final sound of the base form of the verb.

1. The -ed is pronounced /t/ if the verb ends with the sound /p/, /k/, /tʃ/, /f/, /s/, /ʃ/, or /ks/.
   work – worked /wɔrkt/   wash – washed /wɑʃt/   watch – watched /wɑtʃt/

2. The -ed is pronounced /d/ if the verb ends with the sound /b/, /g/, /dʒ/, /v/, /ð/, /z/, /ʒ/, /m/, /n/, /ŋ/, /l/, or /r/.
   plan – planned /plænd/   judge – judged /dʒʌdʒd/   bang – banged /bæŋd/
   bathe – bathed /beɪðd/   massage – massaged /mə'sɑʒd/   rub – rubbed /rʌbd/

3. The -ed is also pronounced /d/ if the verb ends with a vowel sound.
   play – played /pleɪd/   sigh – sighed /saɪd/   row – rowed /roʊd/
   bow – bowed /baʊd/   sue – sued /sud/   free – freed /frid/

4. The -ed is pronounced as an extra syllable, /ɪd/, if the verb ends with the sound /d/ or /t/.
   guide – guided /'gaɪdɪd/   remind – reminded /,ri'maɪndɪd/
   rent – rented /'rɛntɪd/   invite – invited /,in'vaɪtɪd/

B3 Pronouncing Verbs Ending in -ed

Listen to the pronunciation of each verb. Which ending do you hear? Check (✓) the correct column.

/t/	/d/	/ɪd/

Vocabulary Notes

More Adverbs with the Present Perfect

Never means "not ever" or "not at any time." We can use *never* instead of *not* in negative statements. Do not use *never* with *not*. *Never* comes before the past participle.

She has **never** been to Greece.

Already means "at some time before now." Use *already* with questions and affirmative statements. It comes before the past participle or at the end of a sentence.

She has **already** left.   Have they **already** eaten?   What has he **already** done?
She has left **already**.   Have they eaten **already**?   What has he done **already**?

Yet means "up to now." Use *yet* with negative statements and *Yes/No* questions. It comes at the end of a sentence.

They haven't arrived **yet**.   Have you met him **yet**?

Still also means "up to now." It has a similar meaning to *yet*, but with the present perfect is used only in negative statements. It comes before *have* or *has*.

She **still** hasn't called. (= She hasn't called yet.)

So far means "at any time up to now." Use *so far* in affirmative and negative statements and in questions. It comes at the beginning or end of a sentence.

So far he's spent $500.   How much money have you spent **so far**?
So far I haven't had a good time.   Have you had a good time **so far**?

D5 Using Adverbs with the Present Perfect

A. Rewrite these sentences. Place the word or words in parentheses in an appropriate position in each sentence. Use contractions where possible.

Conversation 1

A: Have you asked Sara to help you (yet)?

   Have you asked Sara to help you yet?
   _____
                                    1

B: No, I haven't asked her (still).

   _____
                                    2

Conversation 2

A: Have you played golf (ever)?

   _____
                                    1

B: No, I've played golf (never).

   _____
                                    2

*• **Vocabulary Notes** highlight the important connection between key vocabulary and grammatical structures.*

Beyond the Sentence

Introducing Background Information with the Past Continuous

The past continuous and simple past often occur together in the same story. The past continuous is used at the beginning of a story to describe background activities that are happening at the same time as the main events of the story. The simple past is used for main events.

Yesterday <u>was</u> beautiful. The sun **was shining**, the birds **were singing**, and I **was walking** in a valley. Suddenly, a UFO <u>landed</u> on the ground. Three small green men <u>appeared</u>. They <u>took</u> my hand and <u>said</u>, "Come with us."

C4 Introducing Background Information with the Past Continuous

A. Work with a partner. Imagine that each sentence is the beginning of a story. Write two sentences in the past continuous to give background information.

1. The beach was gorgeous. The sun was shining on the water. The waves
   were moving quickly.

2. The bank was full of customers. _____
   _____

3. The students were late to class. _____
   _____

4. My boss was very angry. _____

Informally Speaking

Reduced Forms of *Have* and *Has*

Look at the cartoon and listen to the conversation. How is the underlined form in the cartoon different from what you hear?

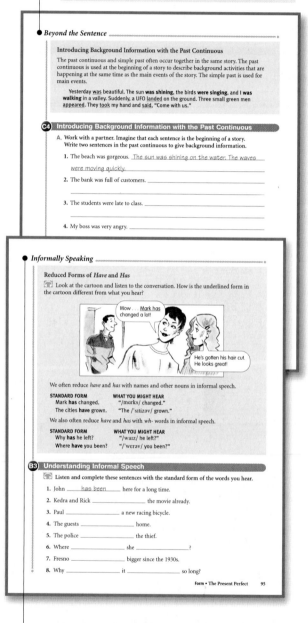

Wow . . . <u>Mark has</u> changed a lot!

He's gotten his hair cut. He looks great!

We often reduce *have* and *has* with names and other nouns in informal speech.

STANDARD FORM	WHAT YOU MIGHT HEAR
Mark **has** changed.	"/mɑrks/ changed."
The cities **have** grown.	"The /'sɪtiːzəv/ grown."

We also often reduce *have* and *has* with *wh-* words in informal speech.

STANDARD FORM	WHAT YOU MIGHT HEAR
Why **has** he left?	"/waɪz/ he left?"
Where **have** you been?	"/'wɛrəv/ you been?"

B3 Understanding Informal Speech

Listen and complete these sentences with the standard form of the words you hear.

1. John ____has been____ here for a long time.
2. Kedra and Rick _____ the movie already.
3. Paul _____ a new racing bicycle.
4. The guests _____ home.
5. The police _____ the thief.
6. Where _____ she _____?
7. Fresno _____ bigger since the 1930s.
8. Why _____ it _____ so long?

*• **Informally Speaking** sections show the differences between written and spoken language.*

The Present

PART

1

The Simple Present

A **Mysterious Island**

Discuss these questions.

What do you think about when you imagine an island? Do you imagine warm weather or cold weather? Can you name any islands that are countries?

A2 **Read**

 Read this geography quiz to find out more about Iceland.

QUIZ

Mysterious ISLAND

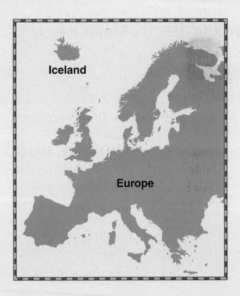

ICELAND IS A TRULY UNIQUE ISLAND—
in fact, it's like nowhere else on Earth.
The interior of this island nation contains
incredible contrasts. It has tundras, huge
5 glaciers, volcanoes, and waterfalls.

Read these amazing facts about Iceland.
Then guess the answers to the questions.
Check your guesses on page 5.

1
Swimsuit maker Speedo® <u>sells</u> a very large
10 number of bathing suits in Iceland. Is it
warm here all year?

2
The island's climate is cool, but most people
don't pay much money for heat. Energy is
very cheap and it doesn't cause pollution.
15 What kind of energy do Icelanders use?

3
Icelanders <u>eat</u> fresh fruit and vegetables
all year, but they rarely buy them from
other countries. Where do they get them?

4
Icelanders like to play golf all night during
20 the summer. How do they see the ball?

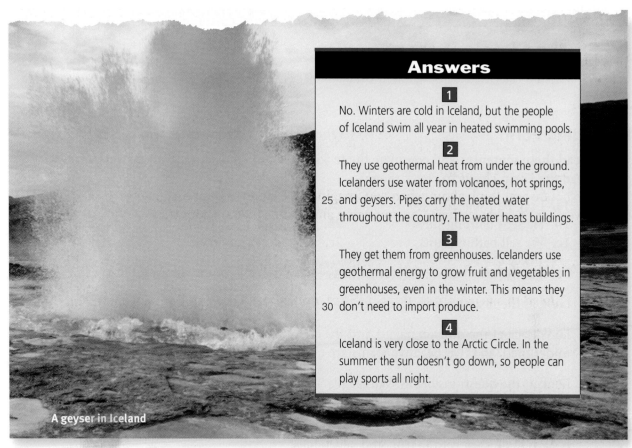

Answers

1

No. Winters are cold in Iceland, but the people of Iceland swim all year in heated swimming pools.

2

They use geothermal heat from under the ground.
25 Icelanders use water from volcanoes, hot springs, and geysers. Pipes carry the heated water throughout the country. The water heats buildings.

3

They get them from greenhouses. Icelanders use geothermal energy to grow fruit and vegetables in greenhouses, even in the winter. This means they
30 don't need to import produce.

4

Iceland is very close to the Arctic Circle. In the summer the sun doesn't go down, so people can play sports all night.

A geyser in Iceland

Adapted from *The Christian Science Monitor*

---

climate: the typical weather conditions of a place
geyser: a hot spring that shoots water into the air
glacier: a large body of ice that moves slowly over land
greenhouse: a glass building used for growing plants

produce: foods such as fruit and vegetables
tundra: a large, flat area of frozen land without trees
volcano: a mountain from which hot melted rock, gas, smoke, and ash can escape from a hole in its top

 After You Read

Write *T* for true or *F* for false for each statement.

__F__ **1.** Iceland is warm in the winter.

_____ **2.** Icelanders use geothermal energy.

_____ **3.** Geothermal energy comes from the sun.

_____ **4.** Icelanders heat their houses with oil.

_____ **5.** Icelanders don't grow fresh fruit.

_____ **6.** The sun shines all night in Iceland in the summer.

B | The Simple Present

Examining Form

Read these sentences and complete the tasks below. Then discuss your answers and read the Form charts to check them.

1a. I <u>sell</u> bathing suits.   **2a.** You <u>don't buy</u> fruit.
1b. He <u>sells</u> bathing suits.   **2b.** She <u>doesn't buy</u> fruit.
1c. We <u>sell</u> bathing suits.   **2c.** They <u>don't buy</u> fruit.

1. Look at the affirmative verb forms in 1a–1c. What is different about the form in 1b?

2. Look at the negative verb forms in 2a–2c. What is different about the form in 2b?

3. Look back at the quiz on page 4 and the answers on page 5. Two affirmative forms are underlined, and two negative forms are circled. Find two more examples of each form.

4. Look at the questions below. Which is a *Yes/No* question? Which is an information question? How are they different? How are they the same?

   a. Does it snow in the winter?
   b. Where do they get the fruit and vegetables?

	Affirmative Statements	
SUBJECT	**BASE FORM OF VERB or BASE FORM OF VERB + -S/-ES**	
I	eat	
You	eat	
He She It	eats	fresh fruit.
We	eat	
You	eat	
They	eat	

	Negative Statements		
SUBJECT	**DO/DOES + NOT**	**BASE FORM OF VERB**	
I	do not don't		
You	do not don't		
He She It	does not doesn't	eat	fresh fruit.
We	do not don't		
You	do not don't		
They	do not don't		

Yes/No Questions			
DO/DOES	SUBJECT	BASE FORM OF VERB	
Do	you		
Does	she	**eat**	fresh fruit?
Do	they		

Short Answers					
YES	SUBJECT	DO/DOES	NO	SUBJECT	DO/DOES + NOT
	I	**do.**		I	**don't.**
Yes,	she	**does.**	**No,**	she	**doesn't.**
	they	**do.**		they	**don't.**

Information Questions				
WH- WORD	DO/DOES	SUBJECT	BASE FORM OF VERB	
Who	**do**	you	**teach**	on Tuesdays?
What	**does**	he	**eat?**	
When				
Where	**do**	they	**travel**	in the winter?
Why				
How				

WH- WORD (SUBJECT)			BASE FORM OF VERB + -S/-ES	
Who			**works**	on Tuesdays?
What			**happens**	there?

- In affirmative statements, add -s or -es to the base form of the verb when the subject is third-person singular (*he, she,* or *it*). See Appendices 1 and 2 for the spelling and pronunciation of verbs ending in -s and -es.

- Use *does* in negative statements and questions when the subject is third-person singular. For all other persons, use *do*.

  She **doesn't play** golf.   I **don't play** golf.

  Does he **play** golf?   **Do** they **play** golf?

⚠️ Do not use *do* or *does* in information questions when *who* or *what* is the subject.

  Who **lives** here?   *Who does live here. (INCORRECT)

- *Have* and *be* are irregular in the simple present.

  I **have** a problem.   She **has** a red car.   We **have** dinner at 6:00.

  I **am** busy.   He **is** a musician.   They **are** home.

⚠️ Do not use *do/does* in negative statements or in questions with *be*.

  You **aren't** late.   **Is** he ready?

🎧 Listen to this paragraph. Write the verb forms you hear.

Many people in Hawaii ___live___ in two different worlds—the world of
₁

traditional Hawaiian culture and the world of modern American culture. Keenan

Kanaeholo _____ a typical Hawaiian. He _____ on the island of
₂ ₃

Oahu. Like many Hawaiians, Keenan _____ two languages. At home he and
₄

his family _____ English. They _____ to each other in Hawaiian.
₅ ₆

Keenan _____ in a large hotel. At work he _____ English. Keenan's
₇ ₈

wife, Emeha, _____ in the hotel. She _____ at an elementary school.
₉ ₁₀

Both Keenan and Emeha _____ to dance. They _____ to discos on
₁₁ ₁₂

the weekends. Emeha also _____ the hula, but Keenan _____ .
₁₃ ₁₄

Complete this paragraph with the correct form of the verbs in parentheses. Use
contractions where possible.

An okapi ___looks___ (look) like the child of
₁

a zebra and a giraffe, but it _____ (not/be).
₂

It _____ (have) stripes like a zebra, and it
₃

_____ (have) a body like a giraffe. The
₄

okapi's stripes _____ (hide) it from its
₅

enemies. The okapi _____ (be) a relative
₆

of the giraffe, but it _____ (not/have)
₇

a long neck. It _____ (not/need) one
₈

to find food because it _____ (eat) fruit
₉

and leaves near the ground. Okapis _____ (play) in a strange way. They
₁₀

_____ (put) their heads down, _____ (move) their tails, and
₁₁ ₁₂

_____ (run) in circles. Okapis _____ (live) only in Central Africa
₁₃ ₁₄

and _____ (be) very rare.
₁₅

Pronunciation Notes

Pronunciation of Verbs Ending in -s or -es

The letters -s or -es at the end of third-person singular verbs are pronounced in three different ways, depending on the final sound of the base form of the verb.

1. The -s or -es is pronounced /s/ if the base form of the verb ends with the sound /p/, /t/, /k/, or /f/.

   stop – stops /stɑps/   like – likes /laɪks/   laugh – laughs /læfs/

2. The -s or -es is pronounced /z/ if the base form of the verb ends with the sound /b/, /d/, /g/, /v/, /ð/, /m/, /n/, /ŋ/, /l/, /r/, or a vowel sound.

   leave – leaves /livz/   run – runs /rʌnz/   go – goes /goʊz/

3. The -es is pronounced /ɪz/ if the base form of the verb ends with the sound /s/, /z/, /ʃ/, /ʒ/, /tʃ/, /dʒ/, or /ks/. This adds an extra syllable to the word.

   notice – notices /'noʊt̬əsɪz/   buzz – buzzes /'bʌzɪz/   watch – watches /'watʃɪz/

B3 Pronouncing Verbs Ending in -s or -es

A. 🎧 Listen to the pronunciation of each verb. What ending do you hear? Check (✓) the correct column.

		/s/	/z/	/ɪz/
1.	lives		✓	
2.	practices			
3.	works			
4.	closes			
5.	arranges			
6.	tells			

B. Work with a partner. Take turns reading these sentences aloud. Be sure to pronounce the verb endings correctly.

1. Pablo lives in San Diego.
2. The team practices every day.
3. The computer works just fine.
4. My mother closes the window at night.
5. Tony arranges all the meetings.
6. Sara tells everyone's secrets.

Forming *Yes/No* Questions

A. Use these words and phrases to form *Yes/No* questions. Punctuate your sentences correctly.

1. study/do/a lot/you <u>Do you study a lot?</u>

2. teacher/does/your/speak/language/your _____

3. have/do/homework/you/a lot of _____

4. a/do/use/you/dictionary _____

5. speak/you/do/English/of/class/outside _____

6. your/computers/school/does/have _____

B. Work with a partner. Take turns asking and answering the questions in part A.

A: Do you study a lot?
B: Yes, I do. OR *No, I don't.*

Changing Statements into Questions

A. Write an information question about each underlined word or phrase.

1. <u>Water</u> freezes at 32° Fahrenheit. <u>What freezes at 32° Fahrenheit?</u>

2. <u>Kim</u> has a test today. _____

3. A power plant makes <u>electricity</u>. _____

4. Niagara Falls is <u>in North America</u>. _____

5. <u>Dan</u> drives Lee to school every day. _____

6. Dan drives <u>Lee</u> to school every day. _____

7. It is hot in Chicago <u>in the summer</u>. _____

8. The eucalyptus tree is from <u>Australia</u>. _____

B. In your notebook, write a *Yes/No* question about each sentence in part A.

Does water freeze at 32° Fahrenheit?

The Simple Present

Examining Meaning and Use

Read the sentences and answer the questions below. Then discuss your answers and read the Meaning and Use Notes to check them.

 a. Thailand has three seasons: a hot season, a cold season, and a rainy season.
 b. Maria doesn't like her new roommate.
 c. My teacher always arrives at school before class starts.

1. Which sentence talks about a repeated activity? _ C

2. Which sentence talks about factual information that you can find in a book? _ a

3. Which sentence talks about a feeling? _ b

Meaning and Use Notes

> ### Repeated Activities
>
> **1** Use the simple present to talk about activities that happen repeatedly (again and again). These events can be personal habits or routines (for example, activities at home or at work), or scheduled events.
>
> | *Habits or Routines* | *Scheduled Events* |
> |---|---|
> | I always **eat** cereal for breakfast. | School **starts** at 8:00 and **finishes** at 3:00. |
> | He **takes** the bus to work every day. | The club **meets** in the library every Friday. |

> ### Factual Information
>
> **2** Use the simple present to talk about factual information, such as general truths, scientific facts, or definitions.
>
> | *General Truths* | *Definitions* |
> |---|---|
> | Doctors **study** for many years. | The word *brilliant* **means** "very intelligent." |
>
> *Scientific Facts*
> Iceland **has** more than 100 volcanoes.

(Continued on page 12)

3 Use the simple present with stative verbs (verbs that do not express action) to talk about states or conditions, such as physical descriptions, feelings, relationships, knowledge, beliefs, or possession. Some common stative verbs are *be, have, seem, like, want, know, understand, mean, believe, own,* and *belong.* See Appendix 7 for a list of common stative verbs.

He **is** tall and **has** dark hair.   She **knows** the answer.

She **seems** angry.   I don't **understand**.

You **like** sports.   I **believe** you.

They **want** a new car.   We **belong** to the soccer club.

4 Use adverbs of frequency with the simple present to express how often something happens. Adverbs of frequency usually come before the main verb, but after the verb *be*.

She **always** has ballet from 3:00 to 6:00 P.M.

The cafeteria food is **usually** bad.

My mother **often** cooks for us.

It **sometimes** rains here in the summer.

My brother and I **seldom** fight.

He **never** cleans his room.

C1 Listening for Meaning and Use ▶ Notes 1, 2

Listen to each statement. Is the speaker describing a personal routine or a general truth? Check (✓) the correct column.

	PERSONAL ROUTINE	GENERAL TRUTH
1.		✓
2.	✓	
3.		✓
4.	✓	
5.	✓	
6.		✓

A. Read these statements. Check (✓) the ones that are true for you.

   ✓   **1.** I always wash the dishes after dinner.

       2. I often ride the bus in the morning.

   ✓   **3.** My friends sometimes visit me on Saturdays.

   ✓   **4.** I often get up at 7:00 A.M.

   ✓   **5.** I usually recycle newspapers.

       6. I never go to bed before midnight.

       7. My friends and I sometimes study together in the evenings.

       8. I never stay home on Saturday nights.

B. Work with a partner. Look at the statements in part A that you did not check. Take turns talking about them.

A: I don't always wash the dishes after dinner. I sometimes leave them for the next day.

B: I seldom ride the bus in the morning. I have a car.

A. Work with a partner. How much do you remember from the quiz about Iceland on page 4? Take turns asking and answering questions about the meaning of these words. If you don't remember the meaning of a word, look at the definitions on page 5.

1. tundra

    A: What does the word tundra *mean?*
    B: The word tundra *means "a large, flat area of frozen land."*

2. glacier

3. greenhouse

4. climate

5. geyser

6. volcano

B. Look back at the quiz on page 4. Find a word that is new to you and ask your partner what it means. If your partner doesn't know, look in a dictionary.

A. Complete this paragraph with the correct form of the verbs in parentheses.

Bobsledding ___is___ (be) a dangerous sport. A bobsled

___weighs___ (weigh) about 600 pounds and ___carries___ (carry) four people.

Each person on a bobsled team ___has___ (have) an important job. First,

all four people ___move___ (move) the sled back and forth. When it

___starts___ (start) to move, they ___push___ (push) it very hard, and the pilot

___jumps___ (jump) into the bobsled to steer. Then, the person on each side

___jumps___ (jump) in. The brakeman ___stays___ (stay) at the back and

___pushes___ (push) for a few more seconds. Then he or she ___gets___ (get)

in, too. The bobsled ___is___ (be) very fast. It ___goes___ (go) up to

90 miles per hour.

B. Describe another sport. In your notebook, write five or six facts about the sport, using the simple present.

Ice hockey is a popular sport in cold places like Canada and the northeastern United States. This game has two teams of players. The players wear ice skates and play on an ice-skating rink. . . .

Combining Form, Meaning, and Use

D1 Thinking About Meaning and Use

Look at these topics. Check (✓) the ones you can discuss or write about with the simple present. Then discuss your answers in small groups.

✓ **1.** Traditions in your country

_____ **2.** Your childhood

_____ **3.** A party you went to last night

_____ **4.** The geography of a country

_____ **5.** The life of a 19ᵗʰ-century politician

_____ **6.** A vacation you took

_____ **7.** How a machine works

_____ **8.** Your best friend's personality

D2 Editing

Find the errors in this paragraph and correct them.

   Which large American city ~~are~~ *is* on three islands? New York City! New York is on Manhattan Island, Long Island, and Staten Island. Most people thinks of Manhattan when they think of New York City. This is because Manhattan ~~have~~ *has* the tall buildings that New York is famous for. Sometimes people travel from Staten Island to Manhattan by boat. However, most people in New York *don't* not use boats to go from one part of the city to another. Large bridges connects *don't* the islands. Trains and cars also uses long tunnels under the water to move between the islands. In fact, New Yorkers usually forget that they lives on an island.

► Beyond the Classroom

Searching for Authentic Examples

Find examples of English grammar in everyday life. Look for advertisements in English-language newspapers and magazines or on the Internet. Find five examples of the simple present and bring them to class. Try to find examples with different meanings and uses. Discuss your findings with your classmates.

Speaking

Follow these steps to prepare an oral report about an unusual animal like the okapi on page 8.

1. Do research at the library or on the Internet for information about an unusual animal.

2. Take notes. Answer these questions, and write five or six facts about the animal. Use the simple present.
   - What is the animal?
   - What does it look like?
   - Where does it live?
   - What interesting or unusual habits does it have?

3. Try to find a photo of the animal.

4. Bring your notes and photo to class. Use the information in your notes to tell your classmates about the animal.

Imperatives

A Do's and Don'ts with Bears

A1 Before You Read

Discuss these questions.

Do you like to walk in the woods? Are there wild animals in the woods in your area? Are they dangerous?

A2 Read

Read the leaflet on the following page to find out about what to do if you see a bear.

A3 After You Read

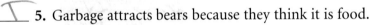

Write *T* for true or *F* for false for each statement.

___F___ **1.** Bears often attack cars.

___F___ **2.** If a bear attacks you, you should run.

___T___ **3.** Bears attack when they feel threatened.

___T___ **4.** Bears are great tree climbers.

___T___ **5.** Garbage attracts bears because they think it is food.

___F___ **6.** Bears are slow and weak.

Do's and Don'ts with Bears

About 250 black bears live in Black Bear Mountain Park. If you run into a bear in the park, it is important to know what to do.

5 🐾 Talk loudly, sing, or clap as you walk through the woods. Bears don't like surprises. Singing or clapping will probably frighten the bears off before you even see them.

🐾 Don't hike through the woods at night.
10 Bears are most active at nighttime.

🐾 If you are in a car and see a bear, stay inside. Close the windows. Most bears will not attack a car, so you are safest inside. Don't get out to take a photograph.

15 🐾 If you are outside and see a bear, stay calm. Stand still and don't run. Slowly move backward. Bears are nervous animals. They are more likely to attack you if they feel threatened.

20 🐾 If a bear attacks you, don't fight. Lie still and be quiet. Maybe the bear will lose interest and wander off.

🐾 Do not climb a tree to get away from a bear. Bears are great tree climbers!

25 🐾 Do not keep food or cosmetics in your tent. Put them in a bag and hang them in a tree that is at least 100 yards from your tent. Bears like anything that resembles food. Remove food, cosmetics, and
30 toothpaste from your tent so you won't attract their attention.

🐾 Burn food waste. Bears cannot tell the difference between food and garbage. They will go after both.

35 Remember bears are dangerous animals. They are very fast and very strong. Be safe. Don't be sorry!

---

attract: to cause someone or something to feel interest
do's and don'ts: rules about what you should and should not do in a situation
resemble: to be like or to look like

run into: meet by chance
wander off: to walk away from a place

B Imperatives

Examining Form

Read the sentences and complete the tasks below. Then discuss your answers and read the Form charts to check them.

a. Bears are dangerous animals.   **c.** Most bears do not attack cars.
b. Do not climb a tree.   **d.** Lie still and be quiet.

1. Underline the verbs. Circle the subjects. Which sentences do not seem to have a subject? These are imperatives.

2. Look back at the leaflet on page 19. Find five imperatives.

Affirmative Imperatives	
BASE FORM OF VERB	
Open	your books.
Drive	carefully.
Be	here at six.

Negative Imperatives		
DO + NOT	BASE FORM OF VERB	
Do not **Don't**	open	your books.
	leave	yet.
	be	late.

- The subject of an imperative is *you* (singular or plural), even though we don't usually say or write the subject.
- The imperative has the same form whether we talk to one person or more than one.
  Teacher to Student: **Sit** down, please.   *Teacher to Class:* **Sit** down, please.
- In spoken English, *don't* is more common than *do not* in negative imperatives.

B1 Listening for Form

🎧 Listen to these sentences. Write the verb forms you hear.

1. <u>Don't leave.</u> It's early.

2. <u>Turn</u> right at the corner.

3. <u>Don't study</u> in the kitchen.

4. <u>Come</u> home before dinner.

5. <u>Don't be</u> angry with me, please.

6. Please <u>don't turn</u> off the light.

B2   Forming Sentences with Imperatives

Use these words and phrases to form sentences with affirmative and negative imperatives. Punctuate your sentences correctly.

1. take/you/your/with/book   <u>Take your book with you.</u>

2. notebook/leave/your/home/at/don't   <u>Don't leave your notebook at home.</u>

3. tomorrow/be/for/test/ready/the   <u>Be ready for the tomorrow's test.</u>

4. questions/to/the/answer/all/try   <u>try to answer all the questions.</u>

5. not/the/during/talk/test/do   <u>do not talk during the test.</u>

B3   Working on Affirmative and Negative Imperatives

A. Read the tips below. Check (✓) the ones that you think are bad advice.

    ✓   **1.** Don't write English definitions for new words.

       2. Keep a vocabulary notebook.

    ✓   **3.** Don't try to use new words in conversation.

       4. Look up every new word you read.
            same

       5. Try to guess the meaning of new words.

    ✓   **6.** Write a translation of every new word.
            same

B. Now change the bad advice to good advice. Compare answers with a partner.

Write English definitions for new words.

B4   Building Sentences

Build ten imperative and simple present sentences. Use a word or phrase from each column, or from the second and third columns only. Punctuate your sentences correctly.

Imperative: *Listen to him!*   Simple Present: *She goes to class.*

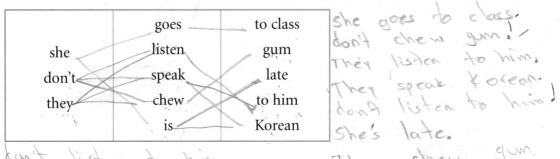

	goes	to class
she	listen	gum
don't	speak	late
they	chew	to him
	is	Korean

She goes to class.
don't chew gum!
They listen to him.
They speak korean.
don't listen to him!
She's late.

don't listen to him
They speak to him

They chew gum.
don't speak to him
she is korean

Imperatives

Examining Meaning and Use

Read the sentences and answer the questions below. Then discuss your answers and read the Meaning and Use Notes to check them.

a. <u>Walk to the corner and turn left.</u> The post office is right there.
b. <u>Watch out!</u> There's ice on the road.
c. Are you getting coffee now? <u>Buy me a coffee, too, please.</u>
d. <u>Talk to the teacher.</u> She can help you.

1. Which underlined sentence gives advice? *d*

2. Which underlined sentence makes a request? *c*

3. Which underlined sentence gives directions? *a*

4. Which underlined sentence gives a warning? *b*

Meaning and Use Notes

> **Common Uses of Imperatives**
>
> **1A** An imperative tells someone to do something. Common uses include:
>
> | | |
> |---|---|
> | *Giving Commands:* | **Stop** the car! |
> | *Giving Advice:* | **Don't worry** about it. |
> | *Making Requests:* | Please **come** home early. |
> | *Giving Directions:* | **Turn** left. **Walk** three blocks. |
> | *Giving Instructions:* | First, **peel** the potatoes. Then, **boil** the water. |
> | *Giving Warnings:* | **Be** careful! The floor is wet. |
> | *Making Offers:* | Here. **Have** another piece of cake, Gina. |
>
> *augue.*
>
> **1B** Although we usually leave out the subject *you* (singular or plural), it is understood as the subject of an imperative.
>
> | *Boss to Employee* | *Boss to Several Employees* |
> |---|---|
> | **Come** to my office, please. | **Come** to my office, please. |

Imperatives and Politeness

2A Use *please* to make an imperative sound more polite or less authoritative. We often use imperatives with *please* in formal situations when we speak to strangers or to people in authority. In less formal situations, especially with friends and family members, *please* is often used to soften the tone of an imperative. If *please* comes at the end of a sentence, we put a comma before it.

Train Conductor to Passenger   *Child to Parent*

<u>Please</u> **watch** your step.   Mom, **hand** me a towel, <u>please</u>. I spilled my drink.

2B You can also make an imperative sound more polite by using polite forms such as *sir, ma'am,* or *miss.* In written English, the polite form of address is separated from the rest of the sentence with a comma.

<u>Sir</u>, **watch** your step!   **Stay** calm, <u>ma'am</u>. Help is on the way.

Using *You* or Names in Imperatives

3 Although we usually leave out the subject *you,* we sometimes use it to make it clear who we are speaking to. We can also add the person's name with or without *you* as the stated subject.

A Roommate to Two Other Roommates

<u>You</u> **sweep** the hall, <u>you</u> **vacuum** the living room, and I'll clean the bathroom.

<u>Maria</u>, <u>you</u> **sweep** the hall. <u>Bill</u>, <u>you</u> **vacuum** the rug. I'll clean the bathroom.

C1 Listening for Meaning and Use ▶ Notes 1–3

🎧 Listen to each conversation. Who are the speakers? Choose the correct answer.

1. a. a boss and an employee
    b. two co-workers
    c. two strangers

2. a. a teacher and a student
    b. two family members
    c. two strangers

3. a. two strangers
    b. two friends
    c. two family members

4. a. two family members
    b. two strangers
    c. a boss and an employee

5. a. a boss and an employee
    b. two family members
    c. two strangers

6. a. a teacher and a student
    b. two friends
    c. two strangers

Look at the pictures. Match the warnings and commands to the pictures.

Stop! Police!   Please put your seat belt on.   Watch out for the ball!

Look out!   Don't step on the truck!   Sit down and be quiet.

1. _Look out!_
men crossing the street

4. Sit down and be quiet.
kids are jumping on the sofa

2. Please put your seat belt on.

5. Don't step on the truck!

3. Watch out for the ball!

6. Stop! Police!

C3 Making Requests

► Notes 1A, 1B, 2A, 2B

Work with a partner. Write a request that you might hear in each place below.

1. (in a classroom) _Please give your papers to me._

2. (in an office) Can you fax this document for me, please.

3. (in an airport) Please all the pasengers with destine to LA it's time to board.

4. (at a party) Please all the children can go to play outside.

5. (at home) Sergio, can you take the trash out, please.

6. (at a movie theater) Miss, can I have two tickets for the titanic movie, please.

C4 Giving Advice

► Notes 1A, 1B

Read each problem. In your notebook, write two sentences of advice: one with an affirmative imperative and one with a negative imperative. Then compare answers with a partner.

1. The light doesn't work.

   Don't touch the lightbulb. Turn the light off first.

   Don't let him alone.

2. My son is sick.

   Don't worry, take him to the doctor.

3. The gas tank is almost empty.

   Don't worry about it, call the P.G&E company

4. I can't sleep at night.

   Don't drink coffe before go to bed. drink a glass of warm milk.

5. I don't have many friends.

   Don't be chy. go outside and meet people.

6. I have a headache.

   Don't listen to music, ley down on the sofa and take (a tylenol) relax. Don't listen to music or watch tv. instead that.

C5 Giving Instructions

► Notes 1A, 1B, 2A

Work with a partner. You are leaving on vacation, and a friend is going to stay in your apartment. Take turns telling your friend what to do while you are away. Use affirmative and negative imperatives.

cat   lights   newspaper   rent   voice mail
dog   mail   plants   trash   windows

Don't forget to feed the cat.
Please walk the dog twice a day.

don't leave lights on during the night.
pick up the mail daily.
check the voice mail every day.
open the windows every morning.
don't forget Water the plants twice a week.

don't rent movies in T.V.
don't throw newspaper away.
take the trash outside every day.

A. Write an appropriate affirmative or negative imperative sentence for each situation.

1. Your friend is new in town. Tell him how to go to the post office.

   Go down three blocks and turn left at the traffic light.

2. You are a bus driver. A man is getting off the bus. Tell him to watch his step.

   ~~Watch out the step,~~ please ~~be careful~~.
   —Sir please watch your step

3. You are going on vacation with some friends. Your mother is worried. Reassure her.

   Don't worry ~~for me~~ about me, I going to be ok.

4. You are a salesperson. Tell your customer to sign the credit card receipt.

   Sir, can you please sign the receipt.

5. You want your roommates to help you clean the apartment. Give each person a chore.

   Sergio clean the bathroom, Vera wash the dishes, Susy vacuum the carpet and I going

6. You dropped a glass on the floor. Warn your roommate.

   watch out, I broke the glass, don't step on it

7. Josh, a close friend, is visiting your home. Offer him something to eat.

   ~~take something to eat~~
   have some fruit.

8. Your uncle looks very tired. Give him some advice.

   rest for a five minutes, relax

9. You are going out to dinner with some co-workers. Tell them to wait for you in the lobby.

   wait for me in the lobby, please

10. You are crossing a busy street with your cousin. Give her a warning.

    ~~be~~ careful, look around.

B. Would you use *you* in any of the situations in part A? Why or why not? Discuss your ideas with a partner.

D Combining Form, Meaning, and Use

D1 Thinking About Meaning and Use

Read what each person says. Is the imperative appropriate for the situation? If it is not appropriate, rewrite it. Then discuss your answers with a partner.

1. (an army sergeant to a soldier) Please get up. It's 5:00 A.M.

   Get up! It's 5:00 A.M.

2. (a cook to his assistant) Bake the chicken at 375° for one hour.

   Please bake the chicken at 375° for one hour.

3. (one stranger to another on the street) Please look out! A car is coming!

   Look out! A car is coming!

4. (a young girl to her grandmother) Sit down!

   Please grandma sit down, grandma

5. (a bank robber to a bank teller) Please give me all of your money.

   Give me all your money!

6. (an adult to a child) Turn off the television, sir.

   Turn off the tv little boy.

D2 Editing

Some of these sentences have errors. Find the errors and correct them.

1. You don't worrying about your memory. *Don't worry*

2. Be not noisy! Don't be noisy.

3. Don't to listen to her. Don't listen to her.

4. Megan, closes the door, please. Megan, close the door, please.

5. Study the vocabulary for tomorrow's test.

6. Leave not now! Don't live now.

Long-Distance Messenger

A1 Before You Read

Discuss these questions.

Do you think there is life on other planets? Is it a good idea to look for life on other planets? Why or why not?

A2 Read

Read the magazine article on the following page to discover the two different purposes of a famous spacecraft.

A3 After You Read

Write *T* for true or *F* for false for each statement.

___T___ **1.** *Voyager* is a spacecraft.

___T___ **2.** *Voyager* is traveling through space.

___F___ **3.** *Voyager* is coming back to Earth right now.

___T___ **4.** People aren't traveling on *Voyager*.

___F___ **5.** *Voyager* isn't carrying pictures.

___F___ **6.** *Voyager* is carrying live animals.

LONG-DISTANCE
MESSENGER

Voyager I is a spacecraft that left Earth in 1977. Its purpose was to explore our solar system. Scientists expected to receive information about other planets
5 from *Voyager* for ten to fifteen years. They were very wrong. They are still receiving messages from *Voyager* today. *Voyager* is currently moving away from Earth at a speed of 39,000 miles per
10 hour (62,904 kilometers per hour). Now it is so far away that its messages take almost ten hours to travel to Earth. After all this time, these messages are still giving scientists important information
15 about our solar system.

Voyager has another important job. It is a messenger from our planet to other planets. *Voyager* is not carrying any astronauts, but it is carrying more than
20 100 pictures of life on Earth and greetings in over 50 languages. It also has examples of animal sounds, different

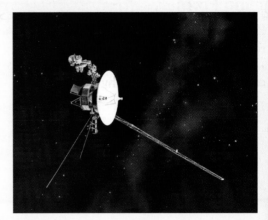

Voyager I

kinds of music, the sound of a mother kissing a baby, and messages from world
25 leaders. In addition, it is carrying pictures of humans and a map that shows Earth's location.

Scientists say that *Voyager* will send messages until the year 2020. Perhaps
30 one day someone from another planet will find the spacecraft and learn about our planet.

---

astronaut: a person who travels in a spacecraft

greetings: words that you say when you see or meet someone

messenger: a person or thing that brings information

solar system: the Sun and the planets that move around it

spacecraft: a vehicle that can travel in space

voyager: somebody or something that travels

B The Present Continuous

Examining Form

Read the sentences and complete the tasks below. Then discuss your answers and read the Form charts to check them.

    a. *Voyager* is a messenger from Earth.   **b.** It is carrying pictures of humans.

1. Underline the verbs. Which is simple present? Which is present continuous?

2. How many words are necessary to form the present continuous? What ending is added to the base form of the verb? *3 words   ing*

3. Look back at the article on page 31. Find three examples of the present continuous.

Affirmative Statements			
SUBJECT	**BE**	**BASE FORM OF VERB + -ING**	
I	am		
You	are		
He She It	is	working	today.
We			
You	are		
They			

Negative Statements				
SUBJECT	**BE**	**NOT**	**BASE FORM OF VERB + -ING**	
I	am			
You	are			
He She It	is	not	working	today.
We				
You	are			
They				

CONTRACTIONS		
I'm		
You're		
	working	today.
He's		
They're		

CONTRACTIONS		
I'm not		
You're not You aren't		
	working	today.
He's not He isn't		
They're not They aren't		

Yes/No Questions

BE	SUBJECT	BASE FORM OF VERB + -ING	
Are	you		
Is	it	**working**	now?
Are	they		

Short Answers

YES	SUBJECT	BE	NO	SUBJECT + BE + NOT
	I	am.		**I'm not.**
Yes,	it	**is.**	No,	it **isn't.**
	they	**are.**		they **aren't.**

Information Questions

WH- WORD	BE	SUBJECT	BASE FORM OF VERB + -ING
How	**am**	I	**doing?**
Who	**are**	you	**calling?**
What	**are**	you	**studying?**
Where	**is**	he	**working?**
Why	**are**	they	**shouting?**

WH- WORD (SUBJECT)	BE		BASE FORM OF VERB + -ING
Who	**is**		**laughing?**
What	**is**		**happening?**

- See Appendix 3 for the spelling of verbs ending in -*ing*.
- See Appendix 16 for more contractions with *be*.
- ⚠️ Do not use contractions in affirmative short answers.
     Yes, I am.
     *Yes, I'm. (INCORRECT)
- ⚠️ Do not use a subject pronoun in information questions when *who* or *what* is the subject.
     What is happening?
     *What is it happening? (INCORRECT)

🎧 Listen to each sentence. Choose the verb form you hear.

1. **a.** is living
   b. isn't living
   c. are living
   d. aren't living

2. **a.** am trying
   b. am not trying
   c. are trying
   d. are not trying

3. **a.** is meeting
   b. is not meeting
   c. are meeting
   d. are not meeting

4. **a.** am sleeping
   b. am not sleeping
   c. is sleeping
   d. is not sleeping

5. **a.** is working
   b. isn't working
   c. are working
   d. aren't working

6. **a.** am cooking
   b. am not cooking
   c. are cooking
   d. aren't cooking

B2 **Forming Statements and *Yes/No* Questions**

A. Form sentences in the present continuous from these words and phrases. Use contractions where possible, and punctuate your sentences correctly.

1. in Canada/Maria and Hector/live

   Maria and Hector are living in Canada.

2. Hector/in a factory/work

   Hector is working in a factory.

3. not/Maria/in a factory/work

   Maria isn't working in a factory.

4. she/Spanish/teach

   Isn't Maria working in a factory

   She is teaching Spanish.

5. English/Hector/at night/study

   Hector's studying English at night.

6. not/live/they/in an apartment

   They aren't living in an apartment.

7. rent/a small house/they

They are renting a small house.

8. learn/Maria and Hector/about life in Canada

Maria and Hector are learning about life in Canada.

B. **Work with a partner. Take turns asking and answering _Yes/No_ questions about the sentences in part A.**

A: _Are Maria and Hector living in Canada?_
B: _Yes, they are._ OR
A: _Are Maria and Hector living in the United States?_
B: _No, they're not. They're living in Canada._

B3 **Writing Information Questions**

Write an information question about each underlined word or phrase.

1. The rice is burning!

  What is burning?

2. Carol is talking on the telephone.

  Who is talking on the telephone?

3. Ben is reading the newspaper.

  What is Ben reading?

4. Eric is studying at the library.

  Where is Eric studying?

5. Their children are playing a game.

  What are their children playing?

6. The children are yelling because they're excited.

  Why are the children yelling?

7. He's feeling sad today.

  How is he feeling today?

8. They're doing their homework now.

  What are they doing now.

The Present Continuous

Examining Meaning and Use

Read the sentences and answer the questions below. Then discuss your answers and read the Meaning and Use Notes to check them.

a. The earth's climate is becoming warmer.
b. I'm eating dinner now. Can I call you back?
c. I'm taking a computer programming course this semester.

1. Which sentence describes an activity that is happening at the exact moment the speaker is talking? b

2. Which sentence describes an activity that is in progress, but not happening at the exact moment the speaker is talking? c

3. Which sentence describes a changing situation? a

Meaning and Use Notes

> **Activities in Progress**
>
> **1A** Use the present continuous for activities that are in progress (or happening) at the exact moment the speaker is talking. You can use time expressions such as *now* or *right now* to emphasize that an action is happening currently (and may end soon).
>
> *Activities in Progress at This Exact Moment*
> Look! It**'s snowing**!
> She**'s making** dinner <u>now</u>.
> Steve can't come to the phone <u>right now</u>. He**'s taking** a bath.
>
> ---
>
> **1B** Use the present continuous for activities that are in progress, but not happening at the exact moment the speaker is talking. You can use time expressions such as *this week* or *these days* to show when the action is happening.
>
> *Activities in Progress, but Not Happening at This Exact Moment*
> I**'m looking** for a cheap car. Do you have any ideas?
> I**'m painting** my house <u>this week</u>. It**'s taking** a long time.

1C Use the present continuous for changing situations.

Changing Situations
My grades **are improving** this semester.
Computers **are getting** cheaper all the time.

Stative Verbs and the Present Continuous

2A Many stative verbs are not generally used in the present continuous. They are usually used in the simple present. Some of these verbs are *know, mean, own, seem,* and *understand*. See Appendix 7 for a list of more stative verbs.

Simple Present	*Present Continuous*
Do you **know** the answer?	*Are you knowing the answer? (INCORRECT)
What **does** *solar system* **mean**?	*What is *solar system* meaning? (INCORRECT)
We **don't own** a car.	*We're not owning a car. (INCORRECT)

2B Some stative verbs can be used in the present continuous, but they are used as action verbs and have a different meaning from their simple present meaning. Some of these verbs are *have, look, see, taste, think,* and *weigh*.

Simple Present	*Present Continuous*
They **have** a large house. (They own a large house.)	They**'re having** a good time. (They're experiencing a good time.)
Mark **looks** very unhappy. (Mark seems unhappy.)	Mark **is looking** for his car keys. (Mark is searching for his car keys.)
I **see** Lisa. She's behind Bob. (I'm looking at Lisa.)	I**'m seeing** Lisa. (I'm dating Lisa.)
The soup **tastes** salty. (The soup has a salty taste.)	The chef **is tasting** the soup. (The chef is trying the soup.)
I **think** that's a great idea. (I believe that's a great idea.)	I**'m thinking** about Lisa. I like her a lot. (Lisa is in my thoughts right now.)
The package **weighs** two pounds. (Its weight is two pounds.)	The postal worker **is weighing** the package. (The postal worker is using a scale.)

2C Stative verbs that refer to physical conditions can occur in the simple present or present continuous with no difference in meaning. Some of these verbs are *ache, feel,* and *hurt*.

Simple Present	*Present Continuous*
I **don't feel** well.	I**'m not feeling** well.
My throat **hurts**.	My throat **is hurting**.

Listening for Meaning and Use ► Note 1A

Listen to the announcements. Where would you hear each one?

a in an airport   *c* on an airplane   *e* on a train
b in a store   *d* on a ship   *f* on television or the radio

1. _on an airplane — c_   3. ___a___   5. ___f___
2. ___e___   4. ___b___   6. ___d___

C2 **Understanding Meaning and Use** ► Notes 1A–1C

Read each conversation and look at the underlined verb form. Is the
statement that follows true or false? Write *T* for true or *F* for false. Then
discuss your answers with a partner.

1. **Carlos:** Thanks for the ride, Marta. You seem really tired. Are you OK?
   Marta: Well, I'm working a lot of extra hours these days. I guess I am
   pretty tired.

   __F__ Marta is working in the office right now.

2. **Dan:** I need to find a cheap apartment, and it's not easy.
   Lee: I know. Rents here are becoming more expensive every year.

   __T__ The cost of renting an apartment is changing.

3. **Amy:** How's school this semester?
   Emily: Great! I'm studying physics, and I really like it.

   __F__ Emily is studying physics at this exact moment.

4. **Nesha:** Please answer the phone, Nicole.
   Nicole: I'm sorry. I can't. I'm helping a customer.

   __T__ Nicole is helping a customer right now.

5. **Steve:** How's your new puppy?
   Jenny: Don't ask! She's ruining everything in my apartment.

   __T__ The puppy is ruining everything these days.

6. **Minhee:** What's wrong, Hanna? You don't look happy.
   Hanna: I'm getting a cold.

   __F__ Hanna woke up with a bad cold.

Look at the pictures. How are they different? In your notebook, write as many sentences as you can. Use the verbs below and the present continuous. (You can use some verbs more than once.)

chase   enter   help   look   run   shout   wait   walk

In picture 1, the police officer is helping the woman.
In picture 2, he isn't helping the woman. He's chasing a thief.

1.

2.

Vocabulary Notes

Adverbs and Time Expressions with the Present Continuous

Still and the Present Continuous *Still* is an adverb that is often used with the present continuous. *Still* emphasizes that the activity or state is in progress. It often suggests surprise that the activity or state has not ended. Place *still* after *be* in affirmative statements, before *be* in negative statements, and after the subject in questions.

AFFIRMATIVE STATEMENT	NEGATIVE STATEMENT
He is **still** living with his parents.	He **still** isn't living on his own.

YES/NO QUESTION	INFORMATION QUESTION
Is he **still** living with his parents?	Why is he **still** living with his parents?

Time Expressions with the Present Continuous Time expressions are also commonly used with the present continuous. Some time expressions refer to an exact moment in the present. These include *now*, *right now*, and *at the moment*.

Others refer to a longer time period that includes the present moment. These include *this morning*, *this afternoon*, *this evening*, *this week*, *this month*, *this semester*, *this year*, *these days*, and *nowadays*.

Time expressions can occur at the beginning or end of a sentence.

EXACT MOMENT	LONGER TIME PERIOD
Now I'm making dinner.	She's working hard **this morning**.
He's sleeping **right now**.	**This week** I'm doing research at the library.
He's taking a shower **at the moment**.	She's feeling much better **these days**.

C4) Using Adverbs and Time Expressions with the Present Continuous

In your notebook, write sentences about yourself and people you know. Use the present continuous and these subjects and time expressions.

1. I/right now
   I am studying English right now.

2. My best friend/these days

3. Some of my friends/still

4. My English class/right now

5. My family/nowadays

6. I/still

7. I/this year

8. My neighbor/still

Look at the pictures. In your notebook, use these words and phrases to write sentences about the people's jobs and what they are doing now.

Work **Now**

1. Tom/drive a taxi/watch TV
   Tom drives a taxi. Now he's watching TV.

Work **Now**

2. Celia/teach ballet/shop for food

Work **Now**

3. Linda and Kendra /wait on tables/go to the movies

Work **Now**

4. Greg/teach math/play the violin

Greg teaches maths Now he's playing the violin

Work **Now**

5. David/cook in a restaurant/fish

David cooks in a restaurant Now he's fishing.

Work **Now**

6. Ed and Reiko/work in a hospital/bowl

Ed and Reiko work in a hospital.

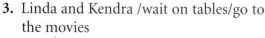

Celia teaches ballet. She's shopping Now for food.

Linda nd Kendra wait on tables. Now they're going to the movies

Now they are bowling.

A. Complete this conversation with the correct form of the verbs in parentheses. Use the simple present or present continuous. More than one answer is sometimes possible.

Doctor: What ____seems____ (seem) to be the problem?
                    1

   Rita: I _don't know_ (not/know). My head _is hurts_ (hurt),
              2   3
   and my stomach _is aches_ (ache).
                      4

Doctor: You _looking_ (look) pale. I _m thinking_ (think) it's
                 5   6
   probably the flu.

   Rita: Oh, no! I _m having_ (have) a hard time at work right now. I can't
                      7
   get sick now!

Doctor: I _m thinking_ (think) about your health right now, not your work.
              8

B. Practice the conversation in Part A with a partner.

Read each pair of sentences and look at the underlined verbs. Do the verbs have different meanings or the same meaning? Write *D* for different or *S* for same. Discuss your answers in small groups.

_D_ 1. a. You <u>look</u> really nice today.
       b. We<u>'re looking</u> at some photos right now.

_D_ 2. a. I <u>weigh</u> 150 pounds.
       b. The clerk <u>is weighing</u> the bananas.

_S_ 3. a. I need to go home because I don't <u>feel</u> well.
       b. Paul says that he<u>'s not feeling</u> well.

_D_ 4. a. I <u>see</u> the boys. There they are!
       b. I'm <u>seeing</u> Jake. He's wonderful!   she's dating Jake.

_D_ 5. a. Nicole <u>is thinking</u> about moving.
       b. I <u>don't think</u> that's a good plan.

_D_ 6. a. They<u>'re having</u> a good time at the party.   They're
       b. We <u>have</u> a new puppy.   experiencing a
                                                      good time

D Combining Form, Meaning, and Use

D1 Thinking About Meaning and Use

Choose the best answer to complete each conversation. Then discuss your answers in small groups.

1. **A:** Stop her! She _____!

   B: What's the matter?
   a. leaves
   (b.) is leaving
   c. leave

2. **A:** ~~Are~~ you ^*working*^ _____ hard these days?

   B: Yes, I'm really tired every night.
   a. ~~Are/working~~
   b. Do/work
   c. Are/work

3. **A:** _____ you _____ their car?

   B: I'm not sure. Is it that green Ford?
   a. Do/see
   b. Are/seeing
   c. Is/see

4. **A:** Why _____ he _____ German?

   B: He's not studying enough.
   a. does/fail
   b. is/failing
   c. does/failing

5. **A:** How _____ the soup _____? *How does it taste*

   B: It's delicious.
   a. is/tasting
   b. is/taste
   c. does/taste

6. **A:** What _____?

   B: My parents. I'm worried about them.
   a. do you think
   b. do you think about
   c. are you thinking about

7. **A:** This package is really heavy.

   B: How much _____ it _____?
   a. is/weigh
   b. does/weigh
   c. is/weighing

8. **A:** Where's Maria?

   B: She's busy now. She _____ the baby.
   a. feeds
   b. feeding
   c. is feeding

Find the errors in this letter and correct them.

Dear Donna,

    I love Sunrise Inn. It is having [~~is~~ has] a very restful atmosphere. Right now I sit [am sit.] under a large tree in the garden. I don't worrying [am not] about anything. The sun shining [is], a cool breeze blows [is blowing], and birds singing [are]. I have [am having] a wonderful vacation!

    What do you do [are doing] these days? Are you work [working] hard? Is Ted still being [~~being~~] angry at you?

Are you have [having] good weather?

    Write and tell me your news.

    Myles

▶ Beyond the Classroom

Searching for Authentic Examples

Find examples of English grammar in everyday life. Listen to an English-language news report for uses of the present continuous. Write down three examples and bring them to class. Why do you think the reporter used the present continuous? Discuss your findings with your classmates.

Writing

Follow the steps below to write a paragraph about what you are doing these days at school, at work, or in your free time.

1. Write a list of activities that you are doing these days, such as studying English, reading newspapers, working in an office, exercising, etc.

2. Write a first draft. Use the present continuous where appropriate.

3. Read your work carefully and circle grammar, spelling, and punctuation errors. Work with a partner to decide how to fix your errors and improve the content.

4. Rewrite your draft.

    These days I'm studying a lot for my English exams. I'm also cooking a lot of Italian food at home. . . .

The Past

The Simple Past

The Decade That Made a Difference

A1 Before You Read

Discuss these questions.

What do you know about the 1960s? What were some important events? Do you have a good opinion or a bad opinion about this decade?

A2 Read

Read the book excerpt on the following page to find out about the 1960s.

A3 After You Read

Write *T* for true and *F* for false for each statement.

____F____ **1.** Before the 1960s all Americans questioned their country's values.

____F____ **2.** John F. Kennedy led the Civil Rights movement during the 1960s.

____T____ **3.** The Vietnam War occurred during the 1960s.

____F____ **4.** All young people agreed with the war in Vietnam.

____F____ **5.** Hippies agreed with their parents' ideas about life.

____T____ **6.** Relationships between men and women were different after the 1960s.

Woodstock music festival, 1969

THE DECADE THAT MADE A DIFFERENCE

Many people who grew up during the 1960s think it was a very special time. Before the 1960s most Americans used to believe that the American way was the
5 best. People respected the law, trusted their leaders, and did not use to question American values. All that changed in the 1960s.

The 1960s was the decade that made
10 a difference. John F. Kennedy became president; Martin Luther King, Jr., led the Civil Rights movement; and women's groups fought for equal rights. It was an exciting time to be young: the Beatles
15 wrote their songs, and many young Americans flocked to the famous three-

A 1960s peace protest

day Woodstock music festival. But the 1960s was also the time of the Vietnam War. Many young people were very angry with the government. They protested against the war because they did not want to fight.

20 The youth rebellion of the 1960s went beyond politics. It questioned many of the values of American society. This was the time of the "hippies." The hippies were young people who had long hair, wore strange, colorful clothes, and believed in peace. They were not interested in money, and they did not agree with many of their parents' ideas about life.

25 Many things changed in the 1960s. Some of them, such as hairstyles and clothing, were not very important. Others, such as laws about the rights of African Americans and the relationship between men and women, were very significant. And there is certainly no doubt about one thing: when the 1960s ended, the United States was different, and the world was, too.

Civil Rights movement: a series of political and social actions to gain equal rights for African Americans

decade: a period of ten years (for example, 1960–1969)

protest: to express strong public disagreement

rebellion: organized fighting or protest against a government or other authority

significant: important

value: a belief about what is right or wrong

B The Simple Past

Examining Form

Read the sentences and complete the tasks below. Then discuss your answers and read the Form charts to check them.

> **a.** The youth rebellion questioned the values of American society.
> **b.** Young people protested against the war.
> **c.** The hippies believed in peace.

1. Underline the verbs.

2. All of these verbs are regular verbs in the simple past. How do we form the simple past of regular verbs?

3. Look back at the excerpt on page 49. Find the simple past of the irregular verbs below. How are they different from the verbs in sentences a, b, and c?

> make   lead   write   go

Affirmative Statements		
SUBJECT	**BASE FORM OF VERB + -D/-ED or IRREGULAR FORM**	
I		
You		
He She It	**arrived worked left**	yesterday.
We		
You		
They		

Negative Statements			
SUBJECT	**DID + NOT**	**BASE FORM OF VERB**	
I			
You			
He She It	**did not didn't**	**arrive work leave**	yesterday.
We			
You			
They			

Yes/No Questions

DID	SUBJECT	BASE FORM OF VERB	
Did	you	arrive	yesterday?
	he	work	
	they	leave	

Short Answers

YES	SUBJECT	DID
Yes,	I	did.
	he	
	they	

NO	SUBJECT	DID + NOT
No,	I	didn't.
	he	
	they	

Information Questions

WH- WORD	DID	SUBJECT	BASE FORM OF VERB	
Who	did	you	see	yesterday?
What		he	do	
Where		she	go	
When		we	study	
Why		you	leave	
How		they	feel	

WH- WORD (SUBJECT)			VERB + -D/-ED or IRREGULAR FORM	
Who			left	yesterday?
What			happened	

- To form the simple past of most regular verbs, add *-ed* to the base form. If the base form of a regular verb ends in *e*, add *-d*. See Appendices 4 and 5 for the spelling and pronunciation of verbs ending in *-ed*.

- Some verbs are irregular in the simple past. See Appendix 6 for a list of irregular verbs and their simple past forms.

⚠ Do not use *did* in information questions when *who* or *what* is the subject.
    What happened yesterday?

- The verb *be* has two irregular simple past forms: *was* and *were*.

    I **was** at the concert.   You **were** at the mall.
    He **was** a musician.   They **were** home.

⚠ Do not use *did* in negative statements or questions with *was/were*.

    I **wasn't** there.   Why **was** she late?
    We weren't angry.   **Were you at the concert?**

B1 Listening for Form

🎧 Listen to these sentences. Write the simple past verb forms you hear.

1. Dan ___invited___ us to the movies.

2. They _____ to the hockey game.

3. She _____ 20 dollars on the street.

4. They _____ the store at nine.

5. I _____ to work by car every day last week.

6. He _____ baseball for the New York Mets.

7. You _____ a haircut! It looks great!

8. We _____ chocolate cake at the restaurant.

B2 Working on Regular Verb Forms

Complete this paragraph with the simple past form of the verbs below.

believe   carry   listen   live   protest   study   support   want

I was a college student in the 1960s. I
___studied___ history at a university in Chicago.
1
I __lived__ in an apartment near the
2
university with four classmates. Like many other
students, I __protested__ against the war in
3
Vietnam. My friends and I __carried__ signs
4
that said "Peace." We all __believed__ in peace
5
and freedom. We __wanted__ to change the
6
world. We also __supported__ the Civil Rights
7
movement and __listened__ to speeches by its
8
leader, Martin Luther King, Jr.

Martin Luther King, Jr., 1963

Pronunciation Notes

Pronunciation of Verbs Ending in -ed

The regular simple past ending -ed is pronounced in three different ways, depending on the final sound of the base form of the verb.

1. The -ed is pronounced /t/ if the verb ends with the sound /p/, /k/, /tʃ/, /f/, /s/, /ʃ/, or /ks/.

    work — worked /wərkt/   wash — washed /wɑʃt/   watch — watched /wɑtʃt/

2. The -ed is pronounced /d/ if the verb ends with the sound /b/, /g/, /dʒ/, /v/, /ð/, /z/, /ʒ/, /m/, /n/, /ŋ/, /l/, or /r/.

    plan — planned /plænd/   judge — judged /dʒʌdʒd/   bang — banged /bæŋd/
    bathe — bathed /beɪðd/   massage — massaged /mə'sɑʒd/   rub — rubbed /rʌbd/

3. The -ed is also pronounced /d/ if the verb ends with a vowel sound.

    play — played /pleɪd/   sigh — sighed /saɪd/   row — rowed /roʊd/
    bow — bowed /baʊd/   sue — sued /sud/   free — freed /frid/

4. The -ed is pronounced as an extra syllable, /ɪd/, if the verb ends with the sound /d/ or /t/.

    guide — guided /'gaɪdɪd/   remind — reminded /,ri'maɪndɪd/
    rent — rented /'rɛntɪd/   invite — invited /,in'vaɪtɪd/

B3 Pronouncing Verbs Ending in -ed

Listen to the pronunciation of each verb. Which ending do you hear? Check (✓) the correct column.

		/t/	/d/	/ɪd/
1.	waited			✓
2.	walked	✓		
3.	rained		✓	
4.	played		✓	
5.	coughed	✓		
6.	decided			✓
7.	jumped	✓		
8.	answered		✓	

A. Read about the first airplane flight by Wilbur and Orville Wright. Complete the paragraph with the verbs in parentheses and the simple past.

The first airplane flight

_____took_____ (take) place in
1

Kitty Hawk, North Carolina,

on December 17, 1903. Orville

Wright _____lay_____ (lie) face
2

down in the middle of the

airplane, and his brother, Wilbur

Wright, _____ran_____ (run) alongside it. Near the end of the runway, the plane
3

_____rose_____ (rise) smoothly into the air. It _____flew_____ (fly) for several seconds, but
4   5

then it _____felt_____ (fall) to the ground. This 12-second flight _____made_____ (make)
6   7

history, but no one _____paid_____ (pay) attention to the Wright brothers at first.
8

However, after they _____gave_____ (give) many public demonstrations of their flying
9

machine, the Wright brothers _____became_____ (become) famous.
10

B. In your notebook, write three *Yes/No* and three *Wh-* questions about the paragraph in part A.

Did the first airplane flight take place in North Carolina?
OR
Where did the first airplane flight take place?

C. Work with a partner. Take turns asking and answering your questions in part B.

A: *Did the first airplane flight take place in North Carolina?*
B: *Yes, it did.*
OR
A: *Where did the first airplane flight take place?*
B: *In North Carolina.*

Build eight logical *Yes/No* questions. Use a word or phrase from each column.
Punctuate your sentences correctly.

Did it rain yesterday?

did was were	it the party the test Maria you the children they your team	rain yesterday first nervous fun win leave difficult start on time

A. Complete this conversation with *did, didn't, was, wasn't, were,* or *weren't.*

Lynn: _____Did_____ you go to the basketball game last night?
₁

Gary: Yes, I _____did_____ .
₂

Lynn: _____Was_____ it exciting?
₃

Gary: Yes, it _____was_____ great. Maple Valley _____didn't_____ win until the last
₄   ₅

minute. What _____did_____ you and Bill do last night?
₆

Lynn: We _____were_____ tired, so we _____didn't_____ go out.
₇   ₈

Gary: _____Did_____ you watch that new television show?
₉

Lynn: Yes, we _____did_____ but we _____didn't_____ like it. It _____was_____ really
₁₀   ₁₁   ₁₂

boring!

B. Practice the conversation in part A with a partner.

Reduced Form of *Did You*

🎧 Look at the cartoon and listen to the conversation. How is the underlined form in the cartoon different from what you hear?

> Did you forget my birthday? It was Saturday.

> Oh, no! I'm really sorry!

Did you is often pronounced /ˈdɪdʒə/ in informal speech.

STANDARD FORM	WHAT YOU MIGHT HEAR
Did you work yesterday?	"/ˈdɪdʒə/ work yesterday?"
Did you eat yet?	"/ˈdɪdʒə/ eat yet?"

B7 Understanding Informal Speech

🎧 Listen and write the standard form of the words you hear.

1. **A:** ___Did you go___ to the party?
      ₁
   B: Yes, I did.
   A: _Did you have_ a good time?
      ₂
   B: Yes, but today I'm very tired.

2. **A:** _Did you eat_ lunch yet?
      ₁
   B: Yes, I did.
   A: What _did you have_?
      ₂
   B: A burger and fries.

3. **A:** _did you stay_ home last night?
      ₁
   B: No, I went to a movie.
   A: _did you like_ it?
      ₂
   B: No, it wasn't very good.

4. **A:** Why _did you work_ so late?
      ₁
   B: My boss needed help on a report.
   A: _did you finish_ it?
      ₂
   B: Yes, it wasn't difficult.

The Simple Past

Examining Meaning and Use

Read the sentences and answer the questions below. Then discuss your answers and read the Meaning and Use Notes to check them.

a. I walk a mile every day.
b. During my childhood we lived in Morocco,
c. I went to Jake's party last night.

Which sentence talks about the present? Which sentences talk about situations that started and ended in the past? Which sentence talks about a situation that happened a short time ago? a long time ago?

Meaning and Use Notes

Actions or States Completed in the Past

1A Use the simple past for actions or states that started and ended in the past. Use time expressions to describe the time period.

I **lived** in Boston <u>in 1999</u>.   They **played** baseball <u>on Saturdays</u>.
We **went** shopping <u>yesterday</u>.   The garden **was** beautiful <u>last year</u>,

1B The actions or states can happen in the recent past (a short time ago) or the distant past (a long time ago).

Recent Past   *Distant Past*
He **called** five minutes ago.   They **got married** in 1973.
She **felt** tired yesterday.   He **was** very sick ten years ago.

1C The actions or states can last for a long or short period of time.

Long Period of Time   *Short Period of Time*
I **worked** there for many years.   It **rained** hard all afternoon.
She **was** ill for six months.   He **seemed** happy to see me.

1D The actions or states can happen once or repeatedly.

Happened Once   *Happened Repeatedly*
I **graduated** on June 5, 1999.   He always **studied** hard before a test.

Listening for Meaning and Use ▶ Notes 1A–1D

A. 🎧 Listen to each conversation. Listen carefully for the phrases in the chart. Is the second speaker talking about the recent past or the distant past? Check (✓) the correct column.

		RECENT PAST	DISTANT PAST
1.	grandmother died	✓	
2.	walked to school		✓
3.	saw Kedra	✓	
4.	bought the dress		✓
5.	took part in protests		✓
6.	studied French		✓

B. 🎧 Listen again. Is the second speaker referring to a situation that happened once or repeatedly? Check (✓) the correct column.

		HAPPENED ONCE	HAPPENED REPEATEDLY
1.	grandmother died	✓	
2.	walked to school		✓
3.	saw Kedra		✓
4.	bought the dress	✓	
5.	took part in protests		✓
6.	studied French		✓

Making Excuses ▶ Notes 1A–1D

A. You were supposed to meet your friend for lunch yesterday, but you didn't. Use these words and phrases to make excuses.

1. go/the wrong restaurant

   I'm sorry. I went to the wrong restaurant.

2. forget/the name of the restaurant

3. have/an important meeting at work

4. my car/run out of gas

5. my watch/stop

6. have/a terrible headache

B. Now think of three more excuses. Use your imagination.

Work with a partner. Look at the pictures and guess what happened. Use *maybe* or *perhaps* and the simple past to make two sentences for each picture.

1.

Maybe she didn't study for the test.
Perhaps she forgot about the test.

4.

or Marbe he had a car accident
Perhaps he's hit an other
car. her fix it

2.

or Maybe she didn't like the food.
perphaps the waiter gave to
her the wrong dish.

5.

Maybe the child got great
grades
perhaps his brother gave y to
him a advice.

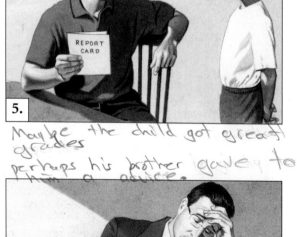

3.

maybe he won the lottery.
or perhaps he went to
the casino,

6. maybe he received a bad
notice.
of perhaps he got a traffic
ticket.

Vocabulary Notes

> ### Time Expressions with the Simple Past
>
> Time expressions are commonly used with the simple past. These words and phrases often refer to an exact point in time in the past or to a past time period. Time expressions can occur at the beginning or end of a sentence.
>
> | | |
> |---|---|
> | yesterday | I saw Silvio **yesterday.** |
> | the day before yesterday | We didn't go to school **the day before yesterday.** |
> | this morning/afternoon | **This morning** she stayed home. |
> | last night/week/month/year | Where did they go **last month**? |
> | recently | Did you move **recently**? |
> | a few/several/many years ago | **A few years ago** he lost his job. |
> | a long time ago/a while ago | Rick graduated **a long time ago.** |

C4 Using Time Expressions with the Simple Past

A. In your notebook, write sentences about yourself in the simple past with these time expressions and the phrases below. You can use a time expression more than once.

a while ago	recently	this . . .
last . . .	the day before yesterday	yesterday

1. write a letter

   I wrote a letter last night.

2. wash the dishes

3. talk to a friend on the telephone

4. eat in a restaurant

5. speak English outside of class

6. go to a movie

7. receive an e-mail

8. take a vacation

B. Work with a partner. Take turns asking and answering information questions about the sentences you wrote in part A.

A: When was the last time you wrote a letter?
B: I wrote a letter last night.

Beyond the Sentence

Using Time Expressions with Tense Changes

In stories and descriptions, we often use the simple past and the simple present to contrast situations in the past and present. We use time expressions to clarify the change of tenses.

Compare the paragraphs below. The paragraphs on the left are confusing because they do not use time expressions to show the change from the past to the present or the present to the past. The paragraphs on the right are clear because they use time expressions to clarify the tense change in each paragraph.

WITHOUT TIME EXPRESSIONS

Sally **walked** home in the rain. She **feels** sick and **doesn't want** to go to work.

I always **walk** my dog. It **was** cold, and he **didn't want** to go outside. So we **stayed** in.

WITH TIME EXPRESSIONS

Sally **walked** home in the rain <u>yesterday</u>. <u>Now</u> she **feels** sick and **doesn't want** to go to work.

I always **walk** my dog <u>in the morning</u>. <u>This morning</u> it **was** cold, and he **didn't want** to go outside. So we **stayed** in.

C5 Using Time Expressions with Tense Changes

Complete these sentences with one of the time expressions below. There is more than one correct answer for each sentence.

last night	now	recently	these days
last week	nowadays	the day before yesterday	this morning

1. My parents rarely leave home, but _____<u>recently</u>_____ they decided to

   visit Washington, D.C.

2. The movie I saw last week scared me to death. _____ I'm

   afraid to stay home alone.

3. My dog and cat are good friends. _____ I found them

   playing together in my apartment.

4. My neighbors are very noisy. They often keep me up until late at night.

   _____ I finally called the police.

5. I was on my college swim team last year. However, _____

   I don't have time for sports. I have too much homework.

6. I celebrated my birthday _____, and Jim didn't even send

   me a card.

D Used To

Examining Form

Read the sentences and complete the tasks below. Then discuss your answers and read the Form charts to check them.

    a. He didn't use to visit his parents so often.
    b. Did she use to like the class?
    c. We used to swim every morning.
    d. Where did you use to live?

1. Underline *used to* or *use to* in each sentence. Circle all the examples of *did* or *didn't*.

2. When do we use the form *used to*? When do we use the form *use to*?

Affirmative Statements

SUBJECT	USED TO	BASE FORM OF VERB	
I			
You			
He She It	used to	arrive	late.
We			
You			
They			

Negative Statements

SUBJECT	DID + NOT	USE TO	BASE FORM OF VERB	
I				
You				
He She It	did not didn't	use to	arrive	late.
We				
You				
They				

Yes/No Questions

DID	SUBJECT	USE TO	BASE FORM OF VERB	
	you			
Did	he	use to	arrive	late?
	they			

Short Answers

YES	SUBJECT	DID		NO	SUBJECT	DID + NOT
	I				I	
Yes,	he	did.		No,	he	didn't.
	they				they	

Information Questions

WH- WORD	DID	SUBJECT	USE TO	BASE FORM OF VERB	
Why		you		**arrive**	early?
When	**did**	she	**use to**	**protest**	against the government?
Where		they		**live**	in Chicago?

WH- WORD (SUBJECT)			USED TO	BASE FORM OF VERB	
Who			**used to**	**live**	across the street?
What				**happen**	on New Year's Eve?

- Use *used to* in affirmative statements.
- Use *use to* in negative statements with *didn't*, in *Yes/No* questions, and in information questions with *did*.
- The forms *used to* and *use to* have the same pronunciation: /'yustu/.

⚠️ Do not use *did* in information questions when *who* or *what* is the subject. Use *used to* with these questions.

    Who used to take you to school?

    *Who did used to take you to school? (INCORRECT)

D1) Listening for Form

🎧 Listen to each sentence. Which form of *used to* does the speaker use? Check (✓) the correct column.

	USED TO	DIDN'T USE TO	DID . . . USE TO
1.	✓		
2.		✓	
3.			✓
4.	✓		
5.			✓
6.	✓		
7.		✓	
8.	✓		

Rewrite these simple past sentences and questions with the correct form of *used to*.

1. They walked to the park every Sunday.

   They used to walk to the park every Sunday.

2. Were you in the army?

   Did you use to be in the army?

3. I didn't go to the movies very often.

   I didn't use to go to the movies very often.

4. He wasn't a good student in high school.

   He didn't use to be a good student in high school.

5. Did your family rent a beach house every summer?

   Did your family use to rent a beach house every summer?

6. We visited our parents on weekends.

   We used to visit our parents on weekends.

D3 **Completing Conversations with** *Used To*

Complete these conversations with the words in parentheses and the correct form of *used to*. Then practice the conversations with a partner.

Conversation 1

A: Where ___did you use to live___ (you/live)?
                          1

B: In Chicago. _we used to have_ (we/have) an apartment on Lake Shore Drive.
                          2

Conversation 2

A: _Did Satomi use to date Hiro?_ (Satomi/date) Hiro?
                    1

B: No, she didn't, but _they used to be_ (they/be) good friends.
                                  2

Conversation 3

A: _I didn't use to like Kevin_ (I/not/like) Kevin.
                    1

B: Yeah. _he didn't use to be_ (he/not/be) nice to me, but now we are good friends.
                    2

E The Habitual Past with *Used To*

Examining Meaning and Use

Read the sentences and answer the questions below. Then discuss your answers and read the Meaning and Use Notes to check them.

1a. We used to walk five miles to school.
1b. One morning the bus didn't come, and we walked five miles to school.

2a. Mary used to swim. Now she ice skates.
2b. Mary swam every day. She enjoyed it very much.

1. Look at 1a and 1b. Which one refers to a repeated action in the past?

2. Look at 2a and 2b. Which suggests that Mary's present situation is different from the past? Which doesn't suggest anything about Mary's present situation?

Meaning and Use Notes

Comparing the Past and the Present

1A *Used to* suggests that a habit or situation was true in the past, but is not true now. Use *used to* for repeated (or habitual) actions or states that started and finished in the past. Do not use it for actions or states that happened only once. Adverbs of frequency and other time expressions with *used to* emphasize the repeated actions or states.

We <u>often</u> **used to visit** my grandparents <u>during summer vacation</u>. We don't <u>anymore</u>.
Did you **use to travel** a lot for work?
She **used to be** unfriendly. She <u>never</u> smiled.
This city **didn't use to have** a subway system <u>in the old days</u>.

1B You can use the simple present with time expressions to say how a present situation is different from the past.

I often **used to watch** TV after school. <u>Now</u> I <u>don't have</u> time to do that.
In the 1930s people **used to get** their news from newspapers or the radio. <u>These days</u> most people <u>get</u> their news from TV or the Internet.

🎧 Listen to each statement. Choose the sentence that best follows it.

1. **a.** Now I'm married and have a son.
   b. I enjoyed having a lot of people in the house.

2. **a.** We added two rooms last year.
   b. Now there isn't enough room.

3. **a.** Now we don't talk to each other.
   b. Now we see each other every day.

4. **a.** We always ate in restaurants together.
   b. Now we eat out twice a week.

5. **a.** Now they don't want to go.
   b. They always complained about their teachers.

6. **a.** I always did everything myself.
   b. We cleaned together every Saturday.

7. **a.** He always cries when he sees one.
   b. Now he's studying to be a vet.

8. **a.** But we changed our minds.
   b. But we decided to have six.

E2 **Comparing the Past and the Present** ► Notes 1A, 1B

Work with a partner. Look at these facts about the past. How is the present different? Write two sentences for each fact. In the first, rewrite the fact using the correct form of *used to*. In the second, use the simple present with a time expression and the word or phrase in parentheses.

1. Few people had cars. (many)

   In the past few people used to have cars. Now many people have cars.

2. Women didn't work outside the home. (have jobs)
   In the past woman don't used to work outside the Home
3. Most people didn't go to college. (many) *Now many of them do it Many*
   years ago people don't used to go to collage. Now Many
4. Supermarkets didn't stay open late. (24 hours) *people go to collage.*
   In the past Supermarkets don't used to stay open late.
5. People didn't move away from their families. (live far away) *Now some of them*
   long time ago people don't used to move Now some of them
6. Most people got married very young. (many/in their thirties) *are open 24 hours.*
   In the past people used to get married very young away from their families
   Now many people got married in their 30 now people live for any from their famili

---

E3 **Remembering Your Past** ► Note 1A

Work with a partner. Talk about your past habits and routines. Use *used to* and other simple past verbs.

A: *I used to play basketball after school with my friends. We always had a lot of fun together, but we were extremely competitive.*
B: *I used to travel . . .*

F Combining Form, Meaning, and Use

F1 Thinking About Meaning and Use

Choose the best answer to complete each conversation. Then discuss your answers in small groups.

1. **A:** Did you go to school yesterday?

   B: _____
   - a. Yes, I go today.
   - **(b.)** No, I was sick.

2. **A:** I went to the soccer game last night.

   B: _____
   - **(a.)** Who won?
   - b. Is it fun?

3. **A:** When I was young, I used to climb trees.

   B: _____
   - a. Did you climb trees?
   - **(b.)** Did you ever fall out of one?

4. **A:** Julie finished law school last year.

   B: _____
   - a. Is she still in school?
   - **(b.)** Did she enjoy it?

5. **A:** It rained here last night.

   B: Really? _____
   - **(a.)** It didn't rain here.
   - b. It isn't raining here.

6. **A:** She didn't use to live alone.

   B: _____
   - **(a.)** Did she like living with other people?
   - b. Did she like living alone?

F2 Editing

Some of these sentences have errors. Find the errors and correct them.

1. I used to graduate from high school in 1997. *graduated*
2. We didn't needed any help. *need*
3. Ana taked the cake to Miguel. *took*
4. Where did they went? *go*
5. He failed his driving test three times!
6. Who give you a present? *gave*
7. When left he?
8. You didn't answer my question.
9. The test were on Saturday. *was*
10. What did happened here?

▶ Beyond the Classroom

Searching for Authentic Examples

Find examples of English grammar in everyday life. Look in an English-language newspaper or on the Internet for news stories written in the simple past. Find three examples of regular verbs and three examples of irregular verbs. Bring them to class. When is the simple past used? Does the article include any forms of *used to*? If so, why? Discuss your findings with your classmates.

Writing

Follow the steps below to write a paragraph about a famous person from the past.

1. Choose a famous person from the 1960s or another time in history. Do research in the library or on the Internet to find information about the person. Make notes about what you want to say.

2. Write a first draft. Use the simple past, *used to,* and time expressions where appropriate.

3. Read your work carefully and circle grammar, spelling, and punctuation errors. Work with a partner to decide how to fix the errors and improve the content.

4. Rewrite your draft.

    Jackie Robinson was a great sports hero. He was the first African American in major-league baseball in the United States. African Americans didn't use to play professional baseball with white players. . . .

The Past Continuous
and Past Time Clauses

A Galveston's Killer Hurricane

A1 Before You Read

Discuss these questions.

Do you have bad storms where you live? Do they cause a lot of damage? What do people in your city or town do to prepare for bad weather?

A2 Read

Read this excerpt from a history textbook to find out about how much damage occurred during the worst storm in U.S. history.

Galveston's Killer Hurricane

Galveston before the hurricane

The worst weather disaster in the history of the United States was a hurricane that hit the city of Galveston on September 8, 1900.
5 Galveston is on an island near the Texas coast. At that time it was the richest city in Texas, and about 38,000 people were living there.

On the morning of Tuesday,
10 September 6, 1900, the head of the Galveston weather station, Isaac Cline, received a telegram about a storm. It was moving north over Cuba and coming toward Galveston. Cline didn't worry when he got
15 the news. Galveston often had bad storms. However, by the next afternoon Cline became concerned. The wind was getting stronger, the ocean waves were getting larger, and the tide was much higher than normal.

On the morning of September 8, Cline began to tell people to leave the island. However, few people listened. Most of them just went to friends' and relatives'
20 houses away from the water. By 4:00 that afternoon, the storm was much worse.

The tide was getting higher and higher when a four-foot wave went through the town. A twenty-foot wave followed it.

Cline was at his house with a lot of other people. While the storm was going on, he was making careful notes of the water's height around his house. Suddenly, a huge 25 wave hit the house and it collapsed. Everyone went into the water. For the next three hours they floated on the waves. "While we were drifting," he later wrote, "we had to protect ourselves from pieces of wood and other objects that were flying around."

Galveston after the hurricane

After the storm ended, the city was in ruins. More than 7,000 30 people were dead. The storm also destroyed more than 3,600 buildings. As a result, the people of Galveston built a seawall. It was 3 miles long, 17 feet high, and 35 16 feet thick.

Today the people of Galveston depend on weather satellites and other technology to give them hurricane warnings, but they still 40 talk about the great hurricane of 1900.

collapse: to suddenly fall down
concerned: worried
disaster: an event that causes a lot of damage
drift: to be carried along by moving water

satellite: a man-made object that travels around the Earth and sends back information
tide: the regular rise and fall of the level of the ocean

A3 After You Read

Answer these questions in your notebook.

1. What happened on September 8, 1900?

2. Where is Galveston?

3. What did most of the people of Galveston do before the storm hit?

4. Why did Isaac Cline's house collapse?

5. What did the people of Galveston do to protect themselves from other storms?

B The Past Continuous

Examining Form

Look back at the excerpt on page 70 and complete the tasks below. Then discuss your answers and read the Form charts to check them.

1. An example of the past continuous is underlined. Find four more examples.

2. How many words are necessary to form the past continuous? What two forms of the verb *be* are used? What ending is added to the base form of the verb?

Affirmative Statements

SUBJECT	WAS/WERE	BASE FORM OF VERB + -ING	
I	was		
You	were		
He She It	was	living	there.
We			
You	were		
They			

Negative Statements

SUBJECT	WAS/WERE + NOT	BASE FORM OF VERB + -ING	
I	was not wasn't		
You	were not weren't		
He She It	was not wasn't	living	there.
We			
You	were not weren't		
They			

Yes/No Questions

WAS/WERE	SUBJECT	BASE FORM OF VERB + -ING	
Were	you		
Was	he	living	there?
Were	they		

Short Answers

YES	SUBJECT	WAS		NO	SUBJECT	WAS/WERE + NOT
	I				I	
Yes,	he	was.		No,	he	wasn't.
	they	were.			they	weren't.

Information Questions			
WH- WORD	*WAS/WERE*	SUBJECT	BASE FORM OF VERB + *-ING*
Who	**were**	you	**watching?**
What	**was**	she	
When			
Where	**were**	they	**traveling?**
Why			
How			

WH- WORD (SUBJECT)	*WAS/WERE*		BASE FORM OF VERB + *-ING*
Who	**was**		**leaving?**
What			**happening?**

- See Appendix 3 for the spelling of verbs ending in *-ing*.

⚠️ Do not use a subject pronoun when *who* or *what* is the subject of an information question.

What was happening?

*What was it happening? (INCORRECT)

Listening for Form

🎧 Listen to these sentences. Choose the verb forms you hear.

1. **a.** are living
    b. were living
    c. was living

2. **a.** wasn't raining
    b. was raining
    c. isn't raining

3. **a.** were leaving
    b. weren't leaving
    c. are leaving

4. **a.** aren't going
    b. were going
    c. weren't going

5. **a.** are . . . going
    b. were . . . going
    c. was . . . going

6. **a.** was . . . crying
    b. is . . . crying
    c. wasn't . . . crying

A. Look at the picture. Write sentences about what the people were doing at Kevin's house last night.

1. Paulo and Dan _were playing music._

2. Alex _He was looking and listening._

3. Myles and Reiko _They were talking on the kitchen_

4. Kevin _He was looking for food in the refri_

5. Kalin and Kim _They were looking at the pictures_

6. Nicole and her dog, Sparks, _Sparks was_

B. Work with a partner. Take turns asking and answering *Yes/No* questions about the people in the picture.

A: Was Paulo playing the guitar?
B: No, he wasn't. He was playing the drums.

Forming Information Questions in the Past Continuous

In your notebook, form information questions from these words and phrases.
Punctuate your sentences correctly.

1. four o'clock/happening/what/was/yesterday afternoon/at

What was happening at four o'clock yesterday afternoon?

2. feeling/how/your/was/grandfather/last night

3. the/this morning/leading/meeting/who/was

4. was/what/Mr. Gonzalez/last semester/teaching

5. you/living/five years ago/were/where

6. Dan and Ben/were/on Saturday/fighting/why

B4 **Asking and Answering Information Questions in the Past Continuous**

Work with a partner. Take turns asking and answering questions with these time
expressions and the past continuous.

1. two hours ago

A: What were you doing two hours ago?
B: I was making dinner.

2. at three o'clock yesterday afternoon

3. last night at midnight

4. at seven o'clock this morning

5. at six o'clock yesterday evening

6. ten minutes ago

B5 **Building Past Continuous and Simple Past Sentences**

Build as many logical sentences as you can in the past continuous or simple past.
Use a word or phrase from each column. Punctuate your sentences correctly.

Past Continuous: *Carlos was sleeping.*   Simple Past: *Carlos had a cold.*

Carlos you Ana and Rose	was had didn't weren't	sleeping call studying a cold early

C The Past Continuous

Examining Meaning and Use

Read the sentences and answer the questions below. Then discuss your answers and read the Meaning and Use Notes to check them.

    a. This morning I walked the dog and then I took a shower.
    b. At seven o'clock this morning, I was walking the dog and my sister was taking a shower.

1. Which sentence shows two past activities in progress at the same time?

2. Which sentence shows two completed past activities?

Meaning and Use Notes

> ### Activities in Progress in the Past
>
> **1A** Use the past continuous to talk about activities that were in progress (happening) at a specific time in the past. This may be an exact moment in the past or a longer period of time in the past.
>
> It **wasn't raining** <u>at lunchtime</u>. It **was snowing**.
> You **were acting** strangely <u>last night</u>.
> I **was studying** at Tokyo University <u>in 2001</u>.
>
> ---
>
> **1B** The past continuous is often used to talk about several activities that were in progress at the same time.
>
> <u>At six o'clock</u> she **was making** a phone call, and we **were eating** dinner.
>
> ---
>
> **1C** The past continuous expresses an ongoing past activity that may or may not be completed. In contrast, the simple past usually expresses a completed past activity.
>
> | *Past Continuous* | *Simple Past* |
> |---|---|
> | At 5:45 Greg **was making** dinner in the kitchen. (He was in the middle of making dinner.) | At 5:45 Greg was in the kitchen. He **made** dinner. Then he washed the dishes. (He completed dinner preparations.) |

2A Many stative verbs are used in the simple past but not in the past continuous. Some of these verbs are *know, own, mean, seem,* and *understand.*

Simple Past

I **knew** all the answers.
They **owned** three cars in 1998.

*I was knowing all the answers. (INCORRECT)
*They were owning three cars in 1998. (INCORRECT)

2B Some stative verbs are used in the past continuous, but they are used as action verbs with a different meaning. Some of these verbs are *have, think, taste,* and *weigh.*

Simple Past

Did you **have** a car?
   (Did you own a car?)

I **thought** it was a great idea.
   (I believed it was a good idea.)

Past Continuous

We **were having** a good time at the party.
   (We were experiencing a good time.)

I **was thinking** about Jenny recently.
   (Jenny was in my thoughts.)

C1 **Listening for Meaning and Use**   ▶ Notes 1A–1C

Listen to each statement. Look at the phrases in the chart. Is the speaker talking about an ongoing past activity or a completed past activity? Check (✓) the correct column.

		ONGOING	COMPLETED
1.	live in Japan		✓
2.	write a book		
3.	paint the house		
4.	fix the air conditioner		
5.	write a paper		
6.	take flying lessons		

C2 **Describing Activities in Progress at the Same Time**   ▶ Notes 1A–C

Think about a time when you arrived late for an event. In your notebook, write about what was happening when you arrived. Then read your description to the class.

   I arrived at the soccer game late. My favorite team was winning. The crowd was standing and everyone was cheering. . . .

A. Complete these conversations with the correct form of the verbs in parentheses. Use the past continuous or the simple past where appropriate.

Conversation 1

Chris: Where were you during the summer of 1997?

Matt: I ___was traveling___ (travel) around the United States.
1

Chris: How? By plane?

Matt: No, by car. I ___owned___ (own) a car then.
2

Conversation 2

Paul: ___Do___ you ___knew___ (know) Takeshi
1   2

before this year?

Eric: Not very well. I ___arrived___ (arrive) at school in the middle
3

of the year. Takeshi ___was taking___ (take) several courses at that
4

time, but we ___weren't___ (not/be) in the same classes.
5

Conversation 3

Josh: You ___missed___ (miss) the turn! Now we're on the
1

wrong road.

Amy: Oops. I'm sorry. I ___wasn't paying___ (not/pay) attention. I
2

___was thinking___ (think) about something else.
3

Conversation 4

Celia: I ___saw___ (see) Susan at the library yesterday
1

Maria: What ___was___ she ___doing___ (do) there?
2   3

Celia: She ___was looking___ (look) for information for her English project.
4

B. Practice the conversations in part A with a partner.

Introducing Background Information with the Past Continuous

The past continuous and simple past often occur together in the same story. The past continuous is used at the beginning of a story to describe background activities that are happening at the same time as the main events of the story. The simple past is used for main events.

Yesterday <u>was</u> beautiful. The sun **was shining**, the birds **were singing**, and I **was walking** in a valley. Suddenly, a UFO <u>landed</u> on the ground. Three small green men <u>appeared</u>. They <u>took</u> my hand and <u>said</u>, "Come with us."

C4 Introducing Background Information with the Past Continuous

A. Work with a partner. Imagine that each sentence is the beginning of a story. Write two sentences in the past continuous to give background information.

1. The beach was gorgeous. <u>The sun was shining on the water. The waves were moving quickly.</u>

2. The bank was full of customers. _____

3. The students were late to class. _____

4. My boss was very angry. _____

5. The cafeteria was crowded and noisy. _____

6. The sky looked cloudy and dark. _____

B. Complete one of the story beginnings in part A. Use the past continuous to add more background information, and use the simple past for main events.

The beach was gorgeous. The sun was shining on the water. The waves were moving quickly. Suddenly, a swimmer yelled for help. A lifeguard dove into the water. . . .

D Past Time Clauses

Examining Form

Read the sentences and complete the tasks below. Then discuss your answers and read the Form charts to check them.

    a. At that time, Galveston was the richest city in Texas.
    b. Cline didn't worry when he got the news.
    c. After the storm ended, the city was in ruins.

1. Underline the verbs. Which sentences have two verbs?

2. Look at the sentences with two verbs. Each verb is part of a clause. There is a main clause and a past time clause. A past time clause begins with a word such as *before*, *when*, *while*, or *after*. Circle the past time clauses.

Sentences with Past Time Clauses

	PAST TIME CLAUSE		MAIN CLAUSE	
	SUBJECT	**VERB**	**SUBJECT**	**VERB**
Before	the storm	hit,	everyone	was sleeping.
When	the house	collapsed,	I	was eating dinner.
While	I	was sleeping,	the phone	rang.
After	the play	ended,	everyone	clapped.

Position of Past Time Clauses

PAST TIME CLAUSE	MAIN CLAUSE
When the house collapsed,	I was eating dinner.
After the play ended,	everyone clapped.

MAIN CLAUSE	PAST TIME CLAUSE
I was eating dinner	**when the house collapsed.**
Everyone clapped	**after the play ended.**

> **Overview**
> - A clause is a group of words that has a subject and a verb.
> - A main clause can stand alone as a complete sentence.
> - A dependent clause cannot stand alone and must be used with a main clause.
>
> **Past Time Clauses**
> - Past time clauses are dependent clauses. They begin with words such as *before, when, while,* and *after.*
> - The verbs in a past time clause and main clause can be in the simple past or in the past continuous.
> - A past time clause can come before or after the main clause with no change in meaning. If the past time clause comes first, it is separated from the main clause by a comma.

D1 Listening for Form

Listen to these sentences. Write the past time clauses you hear.

1. Some people left town _before the storm began_ .

2. The weather forecaster warned us about the storm _before it hit_ .

3. _After the people left_ , the tornado hit the house.

4. _When the storm began_, we went into the basement.

5. The river overflowed _when it rained_.

6. The sky was beautiful _after the storm ended._

D2 Forming Sentences with Past Time Clauses

Match the clauses to make logical sentences. Pay attention to punctuation.

_f_ 1. He went to bed   a. several people were still outside.

_a_ 2. When the storm hit,   b. while I was waiting for the train.

_e_ 3. After we visited Chicago, c. he made a speech.

_b_ 4. I made a phone call   d. when he was taking her picture.

_c_ 5. Before Steve gave Alan the award,   e. we went to Cleveland.

_d_ 6. She closed her eyes   f. before I came home.

D3 Practicing Punctuation with Past Time Clauses

Read this paragraph. Underline the time clauses. Add commas where necessary.

A terrible storm hit last night <u>while my friend was staying at my house.</u> All the lights went out <u>when lightning struck the house.</u> <u>While I was looking for matches,</u> I tripped over a rug. I heard a knock on the door. I went to the door and answered it. A strange man was standing outside. He was wearing a hood. The wind was blowing the trees back and forth <u>while the storm was raging.</u> <u>When I saw the stranger,</u> I became nervous. Then, <u>when he began to speak,</u> I recognized his voice. It was my friend's father.

D4 Changing the Position of Past Time Clauses

Change the order of the clauses in these sentences. Add or delete commas where necessary.

1. Alex saw Maria when he went to the laundromat.

   <u>When Alex went to the laundromat, he saw Maria.</u>

2. While Reiko was swimming, she got a cramp in her leg.

   <u>Reiko got a cramp in her leg while she was swimming.</u>

3. When my sister woke up this morning, she ate pizza for breakfast.

   My sister ate pizza for breakfast when she woke up this morning.

4. It started to rain while I was driving to work.

   While I was driving to work, it started to rain.

5. Eva became a ballet dancer after she finished high school.

   After Eva finished high school, she became a ballet dancer.

Past Time Clauses

Examining Meaning and Use

Read the sentences and complete the tasks below. Then discuss your answers and read the Meaning and Use Notes to check them.

    a. I was taking a nap when the mailman knocked on the door.
    b. I put on suntan lotion before I went to the beach.
    c. We were playing soccer while Josh was studying for an exam.

1. Which sentence shows that two events were happening at exactly the same time?

2. Which sentence shows that one event interrupted the other?

3. Which sentence shows that one event happened after the other?

Meaning and Use Notes

Simultaneous Events

1 Sentences with past time clauses describe the order in which two past events occurred. When the verbs in both the time clause and the main clause are in the past continuous, the events were simultaneous (happening at exactly the same time). *When* or *while* introduces the time clause.

Past Continuous	*Past Continuous*
When I was sleeping,	the children <u>were watching</u> TV.
I <u>was sleeping</u>	**while the children were watching TV.**

Interrupted Events

2 When one verb is in the simple past and the other is in the past continuous, it shows that one event interrupted the other. The event in the past continuous started first and was interrupted by the simple past event. *When* or *while* begins the time clause, which uses the past continuous.

Past Continuous (First Event)	*Simple Past (Second Event)*
When I was sleeping,	the telephone rang.
While I was sleeping,	the telephone rang.

(Continued on page 84)

3 When the verbs in both the time clause and the main clause are in the simple past, one event happened after the other (in sequence). *Before, when,* or *after* introduces the time clause and indicates the order of events.

Simple Past (First Event)	*Simple Past (Second Event)*
I <u>walked</u> past my sister	**before I <u>recognized</u> her.**
When the phone rang,	I <u>answered</u> it.
After he gave me the diploma,	I <u>shook</u> his hand.

E1 **Listening for Meaning and Use** ▶ Notes 1–3

🎧 Listen to each conversation. Is the second speaker talking about simultaneous events, an interrupted event, or events in sequence? Check (✓) the correct column.

	SIMULTANEOUS	INTERRUPTED	IN SEQUENCE
	while	*When*	*before, when, after*
1.		✓	
2.	✓		
3.			✓
4.		✓	
5.	✓		
6.			✓

E2 **Understanding Time Clauses** ▶ Notes 2, 3

Work with a partner. Discuss why these sentences are not logical. Then change the time clause in each sentence to make it logical.

1. Before Carlos threw the ball, I caught it.

   A: Sentence 1 isn't logical. You can't catch a ball before someone throws it.
   B: It should be "After Carlos threw the ball, I caught it."

2. While Ben found his car keys, he drove away.

3. When the sun came up, it was very dark.

4. Everyone danced before the band started to play.

5. After we went swimming, they filled the pool with water.

Read each situation. Then complete each sentence with a clause in the simple past.

1. Silvio and Maria bought a new house last month.

   Before they bought the house, _they saved a lot of money._

   When they saw the house for the first time, _they fell in love with the huse_

   After they moved in, _they were so happy. the huse_

2. Megan went to a great party last night.

   Before she went to the party, _she bought a new dress._

   When she arrived at the party, _she found her best friend._

   After she left the party, _she was so tired._

3. Paul traveled to Europe last summer for his vacation.

   Before _he brought new bagages. he traveled to. Europe._

   When _he arrive to Europe, he was so exited_

   After _he visited same beutiful places, he came back home._

Complete the time clauses. Use the simple past or the past continuous.

1. Donna and I made dinner together last night. While Donna was

   chopping the vegetables, _I was baking a cake for dessert._

2. We were watching the movie when _the lights went out._

3. I'm sorry I didn't answer the phone this morning. It rang while _I was_
   taking a shower.

4. Last night while I was watching TV, _I heard same stranger no ises_

5. At first Lauren wasn't a good student. After _she studied_
   every night, her grades improved.

6. Why did you leave the party so early? We had a great time! After you left,

   we started to listened great music.

F Combining Form, Meaning, and Use

F1 Thinking About Meaning and Use

Read each sentence and answer the questions that follow with *Yes, No,* or *It's not clear.* Then discuss your answers with a partner.

1. We ran out of the building when the fire alarm started to ring.

   _____Yes_____ **a.** Were they in the building before the fire alarm started to ring?

   _____No_____ **b.** After the fire alarm rang, did they stay in the building for a long time?

2. Lynn was sleeping while Holly was cleaning the house.

   _____No_____ **a.** Did Lynn help Holly clean the house?

   It's not clear **b.** Did Lynn fall asleep before Holly started cleaning the house?

3. Lisa saw Jake this morning. He was walking down the street with his dog.

   _____No_____ **a.** Did Lisa walk down the street with Jake?

   _____Yes_____ **b.** Did Jake continue walking after Lisa saw him?

4. Gina was afraid. It was raining very hard, and the wind was blowing.

   It's not clear **a.** Did the wind and the rain make Gina afraid?

   It's not clear **b.** Was Gina afraid before the storm started?

5. Jake was working on the roof when he fell off.

   It's not **a.** Did he hurt himself badly?

   It's not c. **b.** Did he work after he fell?

6. When he left the house, he wasn't carrying his umbrella.

   _____No_____ **a.** Did he take his umbrella with him?

   It's not clear **b.** Was it raining when he left the house?

7. The fire started after we left the building.

_____Yes_____ **a.** Were we in danger?

It's not clear **b.** Did we start the fire?

8. She was unlocking the door when she heard a loud noise.

_____No_____ **a.** Did she hear the noise before she unlocked the door?

_____Yes_____ **b.** Did she hear the noise at the same time as she was unlocking the door?

9. Don was waiting in the car while Helen was arguing with the store manager.

_____No_____ **a.** Did Don go into the store?

_____No_____ **b.** Did Don and Helen both argue with the manager?

10. Mike left before the end of the game.

_____No_____ **a.** Did Mike see the end of the game?

_____Yes_____ **b.** Did the game end after Mike left?

F2 **Editing**

Some of these sentences have errors. Find the errors and correct them.

                        broke

1. I feel terrible. I ~~was breaking~~ my favorite necklace when I put it on this morning.

                             dropped

2. I'm so sorry about your mug. I was dropping it.

         owned

3. They were owning a house before they had children.

4. It snowing when we went to school.

5. While we were shopping, they were cleaning the house.

             threw

6. After he was throwing the ball, it hit the window.

      was he saying

7. What did he say to you while you watched the movie?

            telling

8. Where were you going when I was seeing you yesterday?

9. She was reading after she fell asleep.

10. He hit his head when he had the car accident.

► Beyond the Classroom

Searching for Authentic Examples

Find examples of English grammar in everyday life. Look in an article in an English-language newspaper or on the Internet for examples of the past continuous and past time clauses. Write down three examples of each and bring them to class. Why was the past continuous used? Why was the simple past used? Discuss your findings with your classmates.

Writing

Follow the steps below to write a paragraph about a hurricane, flood, or other natural disaster.

1. Do research in the library or on the Internet about a natural disaster. Take notes. Use these questions to help you.
   - What, if anything, did people do to prepare for the disaster?
   - What did they do when the disaster struck?
   - What damage occurred during the disaster?
   - What happened after the disaster?

2. Write a first draft. Use the simple past, the past continuous, and past time clauses where appropriate.

3. Reread your work carefully and circle grammar, spelling, and punctuation errors. Work with a partner to decide how to fix your errors and improve the content.

4. Rewrite your draft.

   A terrible earthquake hit my country last year. When it hit, people were working at their jobs and children were studying at school. It seemed like a normal day. . . .

The Present Perfect

A   Tales of a World Traveler

A1   Before You Read

Discuss these questions.

Do you like to travel? What are some good and bad things about traveling? Name some countries you have visited. Where else do you want to go?

A2   Read

 Read this magazine article to find out about world traveler John Clouse.

Tales of a World Traveler

According to *Guinness World Records™*, John Clouse has visited more places than anyone else in the world. He has been to 192 countries and almost all of the
5 world's territories. In his travels, he has crossed the Atlantic Ocean at least 100 times and the Pacific Ocean 40 or 50 times. In addition to holding the *Guinness* world record for travel, Clouse is also the most-
10 traveled member of the Travelers' Century Club. All of the members of this club have traveled to at least 100 countries.

All of this traveling has cost John Clouse a lot of money. So far he has spent about
15 $1.25 million. It has also taken a long time. Clouse started traveling 40 years ago.

Has John Clouse stopped traveling? No, he hasn't. He has continued his journeys. There are three places that he hasn't visited yet: the Paracel Islands in the South China Sea; Clipperton, a French island about 700 miles west of Acapulco, Mexico; and Bouvet Island, near Antarctica.

Some of Clouse's journeys have been difficult. For example, while trying to reach Danger Island in the Pacific, he almost had to turn back just a few yards from the shore because the waves were too high. The real problem was that he doesn't know how to swim, so another man had to carry him on his back!

Clouse has never publicly stated his favorite country. He doesn't like to list favorites, but he has said that Kenya and Tanzania in Africa are both beautiful. What place has Clouse visited the most? Paris. He's been there 35 times. Does Clouse feel proud of his world record? Not at all. In fact, he realizes that it's all a bit ridiculous. "Wanderlust is a sickness that I got from my father. After all, if you've seen one atoll, you've seen them all," he says with a smile.

Adapted from *The Christian Science Monitor*

atoll: a very small island made of coral
journey: a trip
ridiculous: very silly, foolish

tale: a story
territory: an area of land that belongs to a country
wanderlust: a strong desire to travel

A3 After You Read

A. Circle the places that John Clouse has *not* visited.

Bouvet Island   Danger Island   the Paracel Islands

Clipperton   Kenya   Tanzania

B. Match each number with the correct description.

_e_ **1.** 100

_c_ **2.** 1.25 million

_a_ **3.** 35

_d_ **4.** 192

____ **5.** 40 or 50

a. the number of times Clouse has visited Paris

b. the number of countries Clouse has visited

c. the number of dollars Clouse has spent on travel

d. the number of times Clouse has crossed the Pacific Ocean

e. the smallest number of countries each person in the Travelers' Century Club has visited

Listen to these sentences. Write the present perfect verb forms you hear. You will hear both contracted and full forms.

1. I ____have worked____ here for three years.

2. We ___haven't seen___ Yuji since August.

3. I'm sorry. Mr. O'Neill ___has left___ for the day.

4. Our class ___hasn't taken___ the exam yet.

5. It ___was rained___ every day this week!

6. Don't leave yet. You ___haven't eaten___ your breakfast.

Complete the chart. See Appendix 6 if you need help.

	BASE FORM	SIMPLE PAST	PAST PARTICIPLE
1.	know	knew	known
2.	get	got	gotten
3.	take	took	taken
4.	buy	bought	bought
5.	leave	left	left
6.	cost	cost	cost
7.	show	showed	shown
8.	be	was / were	been
9.	go	went	gone
10.	eat	ate	eaten
11.	make	made	made
12.	do	did	done
13.	see	saw	seen
14.	think	thought	thought
15.	grow	grew	grown
16.	spend	spent	spent

Informally Speaking

Reduced Forms of *Have* and *Has*

🎧 Look at the cartoon and listen to the conversation. How is the underlined form in the cartoon different from what you hear?

Wow . . . <u>Mark has</u> changed a lot!

He's gotten his hair cut. He looks great!

We often reduce *have* and *has* with names and other nouns in informal speech.

STANDARD FORM	WHAT YOU MIGHT HEAR
Mark **has** changed.	"/mɑrks/ changed."
The cities **have** grown.	"The /ˈsɪtizəv/ grown."

We also often reduce *have* and *has* with *wh-* words in informal speech.

STANDARD FORM	WHAT YOU MIGHT HEAR
Why **has** he left?	"/waɪz/ he left?"
Where **have** you been?	"/ˈwɛrəv/ you been?"

B3 Understanding Informal Speech

🎧 Listen and complete these sentences with the standard form of the words you hear.

1. John _____has been_____ here for a long time.

2. Kedra and Rick _____ the movie already.

3. Paul _____ a new racing bicycle.

4. The guests _____ home.

5. The police _____ the thief.

6. Where _____ she _____?

7. Fresno _____ bigger since the 1930s.

8. Why _____ it _____ so long?

A. Complete these conversations with the words in parentheses and the present perfect. Use contractions where possible.

Conversation 1

Silvio: How long _____have_____ you _____lived_____ (live) here?
                        1   2

Victor: Five years. _____ you _____ (be) here long?
                          3   4

Silvio: No, I _____ (not). I _____ only
                    5   6

_____ (be) here for six months.
        7

Conversation 2

Gina: Hi, Julie. I _____ (not/see) you for a long time.
                        1

Julie: Hi, Gina. I think it _____ (be) almost three years since we last
                                  2

met. How _____ your family _____ (be)?
            3   4

Gina: Oh, there _____ (be) a lot of changes. My older brother, Chris,
                      5

_____ (get) married, and Tony and his wife, Marta,
        6

_____ (have) two children.
        7

B. Practice the conversations in part A with a partner.

A. Build eight logical sentences: four in the present perfect and four in the simple past. Punctuate your sentences correctly.

Present Perfect: *She has been a good friend.*   Simple Past: *She went to a restaurant.*

she	have	been	for a long time
they	has	waited	to a restaurant
		learned	a good friend
		went	English

B. Rewrite your sentences as negative statements.

Continuing Time Up to Now

Examining Meaning and Use

Read the sentences and answer the questions below. Then discuss your answers
and read the Meaning and Use Notes to check them.

1a. Hiro has lived in New York since 1989. **2a.** Rosa has been a teacher for ten years.
1b. Hiro lived in Chicago for three years. **2b.** Rosa was a nurse for one year.

1. Which sentences show situations that began and ended in the past? Which show situations
that began in the past and have continued up to the present time?

2. Which sentences use the present perfect? Which use the simple past?

Meaning and Use Notes

Continuing Time Up to Now

1 The present perfect connects the past with the present. Use the present perfect for
actions or states that began in the past and have continued up to the present time.
These actions or states may continue into the future.

He**'s worked** here for five years.   She**'s lived** in the same town since 2001.

For and Since

Sentences expressing continuing time up to now often use *for* and *since*.

2A *For* + a length of time tells how long an action or state has continued up to the
present time.

I've worked here **for** <u>a long time</u>.   I've lived here **for** <u>ten years</u>.

2B *Since* + a point in time tells when an action or state began.

I've worked here **since** <u>2000</u>.   I've been here **since** <u>Tuesday</u>.

Since can also introduce a time clause. When it does, the verb in the time clause
is usually in the simple past.

I've lived here **since** <u>I was 20</u>.   I've worked here **since** <u>I left home</u>.

C1 Listening for Meaning and Use

🎧 Listen to each sentence. Is the speaker talking about a past situation that continues to the present, or a situation that began and ended in the past? Check (✓) the correct column.

	PAST SITUATION THAT CONTINUES TO THE PRESENT	SITUATION THAT BEGAN AND ENDED IN PAST
1.	✓	
2.		✓
3.	✓	
4.		✓
5.		✓
6.	✓	
7.		✓
8.	✓	

C2 Contrasting *For* and *Since*

A. Complete these sentences with *for* or *since*.

1. Alex has climbed mountains ___since___ he was 15 years old.

2. They've been out of town ___since___ Saturday.

3. My boss has been in a meeting ___for___ a long time.

4. He has worked in Brazil ___since___ last September.

5. That restaurant has been closed ___for___ a week now.

6. I've known Matt ___since___ we were in high school.

7. They've studied French ___for___ a few months.

8. Lisa has lived in New York ___for___ ten years.

9. Keiko has liked Takeshi ___since___ she met him.

10. We've been here ___for___ half an hour.

B. Use these words and phrases to write sentences. Use the present perfect with *for* or *since*.

1. Sue/live/Rome/1999

   Sue has lived in Rome since 1999.

2. Betty/work/at Happy Systems/ten years

   Betty has worked at Happy System for ten years.

3. Paul/study/French/two semesters

   Paul has studied french for two semesters.

4. I/be married/to Kalin/last August

   I've been married to kalin since last August

5. Liz and Sara/know/Celia/many years

   Liz and Sara have known Celia for many years.

C3 **Talking About How Long**   ► Notes 1, 2

A. Work with a partner. Look at the timeline. Use the phrases below and the present perfect to ask and answer questions about Gary's life. Use contractions where possible.

be a U.S. citizen	have a business	live in the U.S.
be married	know his best friend	own a house

A: How long has he been a U.S. citizen?
B: He's been a U.S. citizen since 2003. OR *He's been a U.S. citizen for . . . years.*

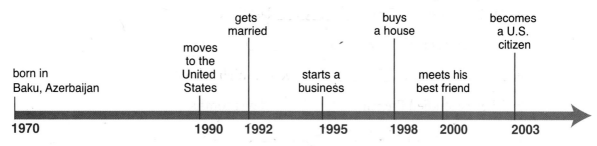

B. Make a list of questions about your partner's life. Use the present perfect with *for* and *since*. Take turns asking and answering each other's questions. Use contractions where possible.

A: How long have you studied English?   *B: How long have you lived in this city?*
B: I've studied English for five years.   *A: I've lived here since 2002.*

Indefinite Past Time

Examining Meaning and Use

Read the sentences and answer the questions below. Then discuss your answers and read the Meaning and Use Notes to check them.

1a. I've flown in an airplane.
1b. I flew to Rome last month.

2a. There have been many car accidents on this road.
2b. There was an accident here yesterday.

1. Which sentences talk about an indefinite (not exact) time in the past? Which form of the verb is used in these sentences?

2. Which sentences mention a definite (exact) time in the past? Which form of the verb is used in these sentences?

Meaning and Use Notes

Indefinite Past Time

1A Use the present perfect to talk about actions or states that happened at an indefinite (not exact) time in the past.

A: Have you met Bob?
B: Yes, I**'ve met** him. He's really nice.

1B Actions or states in the present perfect can happen once or repeatedly.

He**'s visited** Hawaii <u>once</u>.
I**'ve tried** <u>three times</u> to pass my driver's license exam.

1C Do not use the present perfect with time expressions that express a definite (exact) time in the past. When you mention the definite time an event happened, use the simple past.

I **went** to Europe in 1999.
*I've gone to Europe in 1999. (INCORRECT)

2 The adverb *ever* means "at any time." Use *ever* in present perfect questions to ask if an action took place at any time in the past.

A: **Have** you **ever seen** a ghost?
B: Yes, I have. OR
   No, I haven't.

I haven't never seen a ghost

⚠ We usually do not use *ever* in present perfect affirmative statements.

I **have seen** a ghost.

* I have ever seen a ghost. (INCORRECT)

D1 **Listening for Meaning and Use**   ▶ **Notes 1A, 1C**

 Listen to each sentence. Does it refer to a definite time in the past or an indefinite time in the past? Check (✓) the correct column.

	DEFINITE TIME IN THE PAST	INDEFINITE TIME IN THE PAST
1.		✓
2.		✓
3.	✓	
4.		✓
5.	✓	
6.		✓
7.	✓	
8.	✓	
9.		✓
10.	✓	

A. Each of these situations begins with a sentence about the indefinite past. Complete the second sentence with an example expressing the definite past.

1. I've met a lot of famous people. For example, last year I _spoke to Madonna in an elevator at the Plaza Hotel._

2. I've met some interesting people since I moved here. For example, this year I _met the gobernator of CA Arnld sw._

3. My friend has done a lot of crazy things. Last month _she flew a helicopter._

4. My parents have helped me a lot. When I was younger, they _paid all my bills while I was studying at the college._

5. I had a difficult professor a while ago. For example, once _I had a professor who didn't like my perfome._

B. Now write sentences about an indefinite time in the past. Use the present perfect to introduce each situation.

1. _My parents have traveled a lot_ . Last summer they went to California and Oregon, and they visited Florida and Arizona in October.

2. _My sister has been a unstable person._ _he has done many things_ . He worked in a restaurant for one year, he sold cars for six months, and he worked as a bank teller for only one month!

3. _My daughter has danced and sang at musical shows._ _has been in a lot of shows._ . She danced in a Broadway musical last December, and she sang in another show in Chicago this year.

4. _Today I've been very busy_ . This morning I cleaned the house, washed the clothes, and even worked in the garden!

5. _My parents have lived like a gypsies_. They lived in Venezuela for two years, they stayed in Mexico for six months, they lived in Seattle for one year, and now they live in Tucson, Arizona.

I have had a busy day.

Write two *Yes/No* questions for each of these situations. Use the present perfect.

1. Your friends have traveled a lot. You want to find out about their trips.

   <u>Have you ever been to Egypt? Have you seen the pyramids?</u>

2. You are thinking about buying a used car. You meet a woman who is trying to sell her car.

   Have you ever replaced the tires.
   Have you ever had a car accident.
   have you done the smoke test.

3. You want to hire a babysitter. You are interviewing a teenager for the job.

   have you worked with children before

4. You are looking for a new roommate. Someone comes to see your apartment.

   Have you ever paid your rents before.
   have you ever lived with anyperson before
   have you been arrested before before

5. Your friend, Lee, has moved to a new town. You want to find out about his experiences.

   have you met a interested people
   have you gone to the library.

Paul has made a list of things to do before he moves to his new apartment. Look at the list and make statements about his progress so far.

He's called the moving company.
He hasn't vacuumed the apartment.

TO DO

✓ Call the moving company
  Vacuum apartment
✓ Disconnect telephone
  Pack all clothes
  Throw away trash
  Contact the post office
✓ Call mom and give her new address
  Clean oven
  Leave key with superintendent

Vocabulary Notes

More Adverbs with the Present Perfect

Never means "not ever" or "not at any time." We can use *never* instead of *not* in negative statements. Do not use *never* with *not*. *Never* comes before the past participle.

> She has **never** been to Greece.

Already means "at some time before now." Use *already* with questions and affirmative statements. It comes before the past participle or at the end of a sentence.

> She has **already** left.   Have they **already** eaten?   What has he **already** done?
>
> She has left **already**.   Have they eaten **already**?   What has he done **already**?

Yet means "up to now." Use *yet* with negative statements and *Yes/No* questions. It comes at the end of a sentence.

> They haven't arrived **yet**.   Have you met him **yet**?

Still also means "up to now." It has a similar meaning to *yet*, but with the present perfect is used only in negative statements. It comes before *have* or *has*.

> She **still** hasn't called. (= She hasn't called **yet**.)

So far means "at any time up to now." Use *so far* in affirmative and negative statements and in questions. It comes at the beginning or end of a sentence.

> **So far** he's spent $500.   How much money have you spent **so far**?
>
> **So far** I haven't had a good time.   Have you had a good time **so far**?

D5 Using Adverbs with the Present Perfect

A. Rewrite these sentences. Place the word or words in parentheses in an appropriate position in each sentence. Use contractions where possible.

Conversation 1

A: Have you asked Sara to help you (yet)?

> Have you asked Sara to help you yet?
> 1

B: No, I haven't asked her (still).

> No, I still haven't asked her.
> 2

Conversation 2

A: Have you played golf (ever)?

> Have you ever played golf.
> 1

B: No, I've played golf (never).

> No, I've never played golf.
> 2

Conversation 3

A: Has she bought the tickets (yet)?

Has she bought the tickets yet?
₁

B: No. She's made the reservations (already), but I don't think that she has paid

for the tickets (yet).

No, she's already made the reservations,
₂
but I don't think that she has paid
for the tickets yet.

Conversation 4

A: How's the fund drive going? Have you raised any money (yet)?

_____
₁

B: Yes. We've raised $2,000 (so far). We haven't finished (still).

_____ we still haven't finished
₂

Conversation 5

A: Has Rick left (yet)?

Has Rick left yet?
₁

B: Yes, he has left (already).

Yes, he has already left.
₂
he has left already

Conversation 6

A: Have you made any friends at school (yet)?

Have you made any friends at school
₁
yet

B: No, I've been too busy (so far).

No, I've been too busy so far.
₂

B. Practice the conversations in part A with a partner.

E **Combining Form, Meaning, and Use**

E1 **Thinking About Meaning and Use**

Choose the best answer to complete each conversation. Then discuss your answers in small groups.

1. **A:** He visited Sweden four years ago.

   B: _____

      a. Where is he staying?
      b. Did he have a good time?

2. **A:** Emily has worked for the school for a long time.

   B: _____

      a. Is she going to retire soon?
      b. Why did she leave?

3. **A:** I've already cooked dinner.

   B: _____

      a. Can I help you?
      b. What did you cook?

4. **A:** It has rained only once this month.

   B: _____

      a. Does it usually rain more?
      b. Has it rained a lot?

5. **A:** We've been here for half an hour, and a waiter still hasn't come to our table.

   B: _____

      a. I'm sorry. I'll try to find your waiter.
      b. How long have you been here?

6. A: I haven't been to Europe yet.

B: _____

    a. Do you want to go sometime?

    b. When did you go?

7. A: Have you ever flown a plane?

B: _____

    a. No, I didn't.

    b. No, not yet.

8. A: So far I've spent $100 on course books.

B: _____

    a. Do you think you'll need to buy more?

    b. You're lucky you don't need any more.

E2 Editing

Find the errors in this paragraph and correct them. Use the simple present, the simple past, and the present perfect.

Rita and Bob have been the most-traveled people I know. They went almost everywhere. Rita has been a photographer, and Bob has been a travel writer, so they often travel for work. They been to many countries, such as Nepal and India. They have also travel to Turkey, Greece, and Bulgaria. They have see some places yet, though. For example, they still haven't visited New Zealand. This year they've been already away from home a total of three months, and it has been only June. In January Rita has gone to Kenya while Bob has toured Indonesia. Then they both have traveled to Argentina and Norway. Right now they're at home. They were here for two weeks already. Two weeks at home is like a vacation for Rita and Bob.

▶ Beyond the Classroom

Searching for Authentic Examples

Find examples of English grammar in everyday life. Look in an English-language encyclopedia or on the Internet for information about someone's life. Choose a person who is still alive. What has he or she done or accomplished? Find three sentences in the present perfect and bring them to class. Why is the present perfect used instead of the simple past? Discuss your findings with your classmates.

Writing

Follow the steps below to write a paragraph about someone you admire.

1. Write about someone who is still alive. Think about your subject and make notes about what you want to say. Use these questions to help you.

    • Who do you admire?

    • What has the person done? For example, has he or she worked somewhere special or helped other people?

    • Where has the person lived and worked?

    • How has the person influenced you?

2. Write a first draft. Use the present perfect, simple past, and simple present where appropriate.

3. Read your work carefully and circle grammar, spelling, and punctuation errors. Work with a partner to decide how to fix your errors and improve the content.

4. Rewrite your draft.

    I admire my Uncle Tomás. He is a doctor. He has worked with poor people since he graduated from college twenty years ago. . . .

The Future

PART 3

Future Time:
Be Going To, Will, and the Present Continuous

A The Election

Before You Read

Discuss these questions.

Are you interested in politics? Do you vote? Why or why not?

Read

Read this feature article from a local newspaper to find out about four people's opinions of candidates in an election for governor.

THE ELECTION

With the election for governor just a week away, our *Public View* reporter asked people at Westlake Mall the following question: Who are you going to vote for and why?

I'm voting for Greta Monroe. She's the best 5 candidate. She's honest, hardworking, and intelligent. Just think, we <u>are going to have</u> our first woman 10 governor! I am sure that she'll do a great job. For one thing, she's fair. She wants to help poor people, but she isn't going to raise taxes for the rest of us. She's also very interested in education, and that's 15 important to me.

> ***Diane Marshall, 67***
> *retired teacher*

I'm not voting. I used to vote in every election and nothing changed. I'm not going 20 to waste my time anymore. In fact, I am leaving for Chicago the day before the election, so I'm not even going to be here. Besides, I'm sure 25 Overmeyer is going to win. He's not a politician; he's a businessman. He started his own company and now it's one of the state's largest employers. All the business people will vote for him. The others don't 30 have a chance.

> ***Richard Chen, 26***
> *accountant*

I'm undecided. I'm not voting for Monroe, that's for sure. So I still have to decide between either
35 Overmeyer or Kelly. Overmeyer has made a lot of promises, but will he keep them? He says that he is going to help bring jobs to the state. But how is he going to
40 do that? And what kind of jobs will they be? Are they going to be jobs for skilled workers at good salaries, or will they be minimum wage jobs for teenagers? And Kelly? Well, I'm not sure about him, either. He's done a good
45 job as mayor, but running a state is a lot more difficult than running a city.

Steve Corum, 38
unemployed mechanic

I'm new here and I don't know enough about the candidates
50 to make a decision. People say that Kelly will probably raise taxes, Monroe won't be able to do the job, and Overmeyer will
55 only help businesses. I've received a lot of information in the mail about all three. I'm going to sit down this weekend and read it. I hope I can make a decision after that.

Marcy Willis, 28
chef

---

governor: the head of a state government
candidate: a person who people can vote for in an election
running: managing, directing

mayor: the head of a city government
skilled: trained
minimum wage: the lowest amount an employer can pay a worker for an hour's work

---

A3 **After You Read**

Look at the questions in the chart. Check (✓) the correct column.

	WHICH CANDIDATE . . .	MONROE	OVERMEYER	KELLY
1.	isn't going to raise taxes?	✓		
2.	is a woman?			
3.	runs a large company?			
4.	promises to bring jobs to the state?			
5.	is a mayor?			
6.	wants to raise taxes?			

B The Future with *Be Going To* and the Present Continuous

Examining Form

Look back at the article on page 112 and complete the tasks below. Then discuss your answers and read the Form charts to check them.

1. An example of *be going to* + verb is underlined. Find three more affirmative examples.

2. What form of *be going to* is used with *we*? with *he*? with *I*?

3. An example of the present continuous as future (*be* + verb + *-ing*) is circled. Find one more affirmative example.

THE FUTURE WITH *BE GOING TO*

Affirmative Statements

SUBJECT	BE	GOING TO	BASE FORM OF VERB	
I	am			
You	are			
He She It	is	going to	help	later.
We				
You	are			
They				

Negative Statements

SUBJECT	BE	NOT	GOING TO	BASE FORM OF VERB	
I	am				
You	are				
He She It	is	not	going to	help	later.
We					
You	are				
They					

Yes/No Questions

BE	SUBJECT	GOING TO	BASE FORM OF VERB	
Are	you			
Is	she	going to	help	later?
Are	they			

Short Answers

YES	SUBJECT	BE		NO	SUBJECT + BE + NOT
	I	am.			I'm not.
Yes,	she	is.		No,	she **isn't**.
	they	are.			they **aren't**.

Information Questions

WH- WORD	BE	SUBJECT	GOING TO	BASE FORM OF VERB	
Who	**are**	you		**call**	later?
What	**is**	she	**going to**	**do**	tomorrow?
When	**are**	they		**study**	at the library?

WH- WORD (SUBJECT)	BE		GOING TO	BASE FORM OF VERB	
Who	**is**		**going to**	**win**	the election?
What				**happen**	next?

- See Appendix 16 for contractions with *be*.
- ⚠ Do not use contractions with affirmative short answers.

    Yes, I am.   *Yes, I'm. (INCORRECT)

THE PRESENT CONTINUOUS AS FUTURE

Affirmative Statements

SUBJECT	BE	BASE FORM OF VERB + -ING	
She	**is**	**helping**	later.

Negative Statements

SUBJECT	BE	NOT	BASE FORM OF VERB + -ING	
She	**is**	**not**	**helping**	later.

Yes/No Questions

BE	SUBJECT	BASE FORM OF VERB + -ING	
Are	they	**helping**	later?

Information Questions

WH- WORD	BE	SUBJECT	BASE FORM OF VERB + -ING	
When	**are**	they	**helping**?	later?

- See Chapter 3 for more information on the present continuous.

Listening for Form

A. 🎧 **Listen to these sentences. Write the subjects and future verb forms you hear.**

1. _She's going to start_ school next year.

2. _____ home tonight. The airline canceled our flight.

3. Where _____ tonight?

4. Take your umbrella. _____.

5. _____ TV tonight?

6. They hate that hotel so _____ there again.

7. _____ on vacation tomorrow.

8. _____ to the office next week. I'm on vacation.

9. Study hard, or _____ the test.

10. I'm really excited. _____ on a business trip to Brazil next month.

B. **Work with a partner. Look at each sentence again. Which future form is used:**
be going to **or the present continuous as future?**

Working on *Be Going To*

Complete these sentences with the correct forms of *be going to* and the words in parentheses. Use contractions where possible.

1. Soo-jin _is going to study_ (study) in the United States next year.

2. She and her classmates _____ (take) language exams in December.

3. She _____ (not/apply) to many schools – just a few in Boston.

4. She knows that it _____ (be) difficult to study abroad.

5. Her parents aren't worried, because she _____ (not/be) alone.

6. She _____ (stay) with relatives there.

7. She _____ (live) with her aunt and uncle.

8. Soo-jin and her relatives are very close so they _____ (enjoy) living together.

Building Present Continuous Sentences

Build six logical sentences with the **present continuous as future**. Use a word or phrase from each column. Punctuate your sentences correctly.

I am taking a test tomorrow.

I	am	giving	a test	next summer
my friends	is	taking	to Europe	tomorrow
our teacher	are	going	to a restaurant	tonight

B4 **Forming Questions with *Be Going To***

Complete each conversation with a *Yes/No* question or information question.
Use *be going to* and the words and phrases in parentheses.

1. **A:** Is he going to study tonight? _____ (study/tonight)

   B: Yes, he is.

2. **A:** _____ (call/tomorrow)

   B: No, they aren't.

3. **A:** _____ (graduate/this semester)

   B: No, I'm not.

4. **A:** _____ (move/to Canada)

   B: No, I'm not.

5. **A:** _____ (he/study/tonight)

   B: In the library.

6. **A:** _____ (they/call)

   B: Tonight.

7. **A:** _____ (you/graduate)

   B: Next semester.

8. **A:** _____ (you/move)

   B: To Japan.

Informally Speaking

Reduced Form of *Going To*

Look at the cartoon and listen to the conversation. How are the underlined forms in the cartoon different from what you hear?

Going to is often pronounced /gənə/ in informal speech.

STANDARD FORM	WHAT YOU MIGHT HEAR
They are **going to** call.	"They're/gənə/call."
He is **going to** spend all the money.	"He's/gənə/spend all the money."
I am **going to** stay home.	"I'm/gənə/stay home."

B5 Understanding Informal Speech

Listen and write the standard form of the words you hear.

1. We ____*are going to make*____ dinner soon.

2. I _____ to the beach.

3. We _____ him in Seattle.

4. Our class _____ next Wednesday.

5. The store _____ in five minutes.

6. Mark _____ at Lincoln University.

7. The children _____ happy about this.

8. They _____ the test tomorrow.

Be Going To and the Present Continuous as Future

Examining Meaning and Use

Read the sentences and answer the questions below. Then discuss your answers
and read the Meaning and Use Notes to check them.

a. I'm going to buy my father a book for his birthday.
b. I think we're going to have a storm tonight.
c. We're taking a trip next month.

1. Which two sentences talk about an intention (something you're thinking about doing)
   or a plan?

2. Which sentence makes a prediction (a guess about the future)?

Meaning and Use Notes

> ### Intentions and Plans with *Be Going To* and the Present Continuous
>
> **1A** Use *be going to* to talk about intentions or future plans.
>
> **I'm going to study** hard for the test.
> **I'm going to visit** Greece this summer.
>
> A: What **is** Josh **going to study** at college?
> B: He**'s going to study** chemistry.
>
> **1B** You can also use the present continuous to talk about intentions or future plans.
> A future time expression is usually used with the present continuous to show that
> the sentence refers to the future (and not something happening right now). The
> verbs *go, come, do,* and *have,* as well as verbs related to travel, are especially
> common with the present continuous as future.
>
> When **are** you **coming** to see me?
> **I'm visiting** Greece <u>this summer</u>.
> My flight **is arriving** <u>in the afternoon</u>. My father **is meeting** me at the airport.
>
> A: What **are** you **doing** <u>tomorrow</u>?
> B: **I'm having** lunch with friends. Then we**'re going** to a movie.

(Continued on page 120)

1C The present continuous often refers to more definite plans than *be going to*. With *be going to,* the speaker often has not decided on the details.

Present Continuous as Future (Details Definite)

I**'m taking** a 3:00 flight to Chicago. In Chicago, I**'m changing** planes and **flying** on to Miami.

Be Going To *(Details Not Definite)*

A: I**'m going to buy** a car.
B: What kind **are** you **going to get**?
A: I don't know yet.

Predictions with *Be Going To*

2 Use *be going to* for predictions (guesses about the future), especially when there is evidence that something is just about to happen. The present continuous is not used to make predictions.

Be careful! That glass **is going to fall**!

It's cloudy. I think it**'s going to rain** tonight.
*It's cloudy. I think it's raining tonight. (INCORRECT)

C1 **Listening for Meaning and Use**   ► Notes 1A, 1B, 2

🎧 Listen to each sentence. Is the speaker talking about an intention or plan, or making a prediction? Check (✓) the correct column.

	INTENTION/PLAN	PREDICTION
1.		✓
2.		
3.		
4.		
5.		
6.		
7.		
8.		

Work with a partner. Look at the pictures and make two predictions about what is going to happen in each situation. Use *be going to.*

1.

4.

I think she's going to take a trip.
I think she's going to travel to a cold place.

2.

5.

3.

6.

Vocabulary Notes

Future Time Expressions

The future time expressions below are commonly used in sentences about the future.

TODAY/TONIGHT/TOMORROW	THIS + TIME PERIOD	NEXT + TIME PERIOD
today	this afternoon	next Sunday
tonight	this Sunday	next week
tomorrow	this week	next August
the day after tomorrow	this year	next month
tomorrow morning/afternoon/night	this spring	next year
They're arriving **tomorrow**.	I'm leaving **this week**.	**Next week** I'm visiting Ana.

IN + QUANTITY OF TIME	THE + TIME PERIOD + AFTER NEXT
in five minutes	the week after next
in a few days	the weekend after next
in a few weeks	the month after next
in a few months	the year after next
He's going to call **in a few hours**.	We're having a test **the week after next**.

C3 Using Future Time Expressions

Work with a partner. Take turns asking and answering questions with *when* and *be going to* or the present continuous as future. Use *be going to* for intentions and the present continuous as future for more definite plans. Use future time expressions in your answers.

1. you/study

   A: *When are you going to study?*
   B: *I'm going to study tonight.*
   OR
   A: *When are you studying?*
   B: *I'm studying this afternoon.*

2. your best friend/visit you

3. you/finish your homework

4. your friends/have a party

5. you/check your e-mail

6. your history teacher/give a test

7. your family/take a vacation

8. you/clean your apartment

A. Write sentences about what you intend or plan to do at the future times in parentheses. Use *be going to* for intentions and the present continuous as future for more definite plans.

1. (next weekend) <u>Next weekend I'm going to visit my parents.</u>

2. (the day after tomorrow) <u>I'm flying to L.A the day after tomorrow</u>

3. (next spring) <u>Next spring I'm going to study business.</u>

4. (in six months) <u>In six months it'll be my birthday #34</u>

5. (next year) <u>I'm going to buy a car next year.</u>

6. (in an hour) <u>I'll take lunch in an hour.</u>

B. Work with a partner. Ask your partner about his or her intentions or plans. Use future time expressions in your questions.

A: *What are you doing next weekend?*
B: *I'm visiting my parents.*

In six months I'm going to be 34.

A. Think about these possible events. Check (✓) the events that you can plan.

✓ **1.** learn to drive a car   _____ **7.** look for a job

_____ **2.** have bad weather   _____ **8.** rob a bank

_____ **3.** give a party   _____ **9.** have an eye exam

_____ **4.** go to college   _____ **10.** get married

_____ **5.** get sick   _____ **11.** win the lottery

_____ **6.** have a car accident   _____ **12.** watch a movie

B. Work with a partner. Talk about the things you plan to do. You can use the events you checked in part A or others. Use *be going to* for intentions or the present continuous as future for more definite plans. Use future time expressions.

A: *I'm going to learn to drive this summer. My brother is going to teach me.*
B: *I'm watching a movie with some friends tonight. My friend Silvia is renting a video, and everyone is coming to my house at 7:00.*

A. Fill in the chart below with your schedule for the next week.

	MONDAY	TUESDAY	WEDNESDAY	THURSDAY	FRIDAY
8:00 A.M.					
9:00 A.M.					
10:00 A.M.					
11:00 A.M.					
12:00 P.M.					
1:00 P.M.					
2:00 P.M.					
3:00 P.M.					
4:00 P.M.					
5:00 P.M.					

B. Now work with three other students to find a time for a two-hour meeting, a lunch date, and a one-hour work-out at the gym. Use the present continuous as future and time expressions to talk about your future plans.

A: *When can we have the meeting?*
B: *I'm free next Tuesday at 9 A.M.*
C: *I'm not. I'm working all morning.*
D: *What are you doing next Thursday at one?*
C: *I'm not doing anything until three.*

D The Future with *Will*

Examining Form

Read the sentences and complete the tasks below. Then discuss your answers and read the Form charts to check them.

    a. I will decide in a few weeks.   **c.** They will vote for him.
    b. He will probably raise taxes.   **d.** Will Overmeyer keep his promises?

1. Underline *will* + verb in each sentence. Circle the subjects.

2. Does the form of *will* change with different subjects?

3. Does *will* go before or after the subject in a question?

Affirmative Statements

SUBJECT	WILL	BASE FORM OF VERB	
I			
You			
He She It	will	leave	tomorrow.
We			
You			
They			

CONTRACTIONS		
I'll		
She'll	leave	tomorrow.
They'll		

Negative Statements

SUBJECT	WILL	NOT	BASE FORM OF VERB	
I				
You				
He She It	will	not	leave	tomorrow.
We				
You				
They				

CONTRACTIONS			
I			
She	won't	leave	tomorrow.
They			

(Continued on page 126)

Yes/No Questions			
WILL	SUBJECT	BASE FORM OF VERB	
Will	you		
	she	**leave**	tomorrow?
	they		

Short Answers						
YES	SUBJECT	WILL	NO	SUBJECT	WILL + NOT	
Yes,	I	**will.**	**No,**	I	**won't.**	
	she			she		
	they			they		

Information Questions				
WH- WORD	WILL	SUBJECT	BASE FORM OF VERB	
Who	will	he	**see**	at the wedding tomorrow?
What		they	**do**	later?

WH- WORD (SUBJECT)	WILL		BASE FORM OF VERB	
Who	will		**leave**	first?
What			**happen**	next?

- Use the same form of *will* with every subject. See Appendix 16 for contractions with *will*.
- Do not use contractions with affirmative short answers.
    Yes, I **will.**   *Yes, I'll. (INCORRECT)

D1 **Listening for Form**

Listen to each sentence. Which form is used to talk about the future: *be going to*, the present continuous, or *will*? Check (✓) the correct column.

	BE GOING TO	PRESENT CONTINUOUS	WILL
1.	✓		
2.			
3.			
4.			
5.			
6.			
7.			
8.			

Complete these conversations with the words in parentheses and *will* or *won't*. Use contractions where possible. Then practice the conversations with a partner.

Conversation 1

Susan: I don't believe all these predictions. In the next ten years
_____we won't have_____ (we/not/have) hydrogen-powered cars.
1

Bob: Oh, I think _____we will_____ (we).
2

Conversation 2

Jenny: ___will we be___ (we/be) friends in five years?
1

Keiko: Of course, ___we will___ (we/be) friends.
2

Conversation 3

Lauren: Take your jacket or ___you will be___ (you/be) cold.
1

Dan: No, ___I won't___ (I/not). It's not cold outside.
2

Conversation 4

Paul: ___I'll do___ (I/do) my homework in the morning. I
1
promise, Mom.

Mom: No, ___you won't___ (you/not). You're always too tired in the
2
morning. Do it now.

Conversation 5

Carol: ___I'll never learn___ (I/never/learn) how to program this new VCR.
1

Betty: I have the same one. ___I'll___ (I/show) you.
2

Conversation 6

Robin: Do you think ___you will find___ (you/find) an apartment in
1
San Francisco?

Kedra: That's a good question. ___It'll be___ (it/be) difficult.
2
Maybe ___I'll try___ (I/try) Oakland, too.
3

A. Imagine that this is the first day of your new English class. You are feeling very nervous. Use these phrases to write *Yes/No* questions to ask your teacher. Use *will* in your questions.

1. (get homework every night) <u>Will we get homework every night?</u>

2. (have a final exam) Will we have a final exam?

3. (get grades for class participation) Will we get grades for class p

4. (use a textbook) Will we use a textbook?

5. (have a lot of tests) We'll have a lot of tests

6. (use the language lab) we'll use the language lab

B. Work with a partner. Think of two more questions to ask your teacher.

Will we use the Internet in class?

C. Take turns asking and answering the questions in parts A and B.

A: Will we get homework every night?
B: Yes, you will. It will help you a lot.

Build six logical information questions with *will*. Use each *wh-* word at least once. Remember that *wh-* (subject) questions do not need an item from the third column. Punctuate your sentences correctly.

What will you talk about at the meeting?

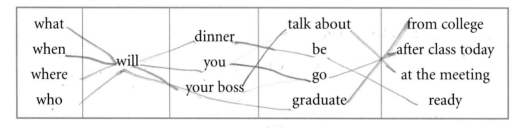

what			talk about	from college
when	will	dinner	be	after class today
where		you	go	at the meeting
who		your boss	graduate	ready

Informally Speaking

🎧 Reduced Form of *Will*

Look at the cartoon and listen to the conversation. How are the underlined forms in the cartoon different from what you hear?

Who will pick up the kids from school?

I will. My boss will let me leave early.

Will is often contracted with nouns and *wh-* words in informal speech.

STANDARD FORM	WHAT YOU MIGHT HEAR
Jake will be late.	"/'dʒeɪkəl/ be late."
The **children will** be here soon.	"The /'tʃɪldrənəl/ be here."
How will you get to Boston?	"/'haʊəl/ you get to Boston?"
Where will you live?	"/'wɛrəl/ you live?"

D5 Understanding Informal Speech

🎧 Listen and write the standard form of the words you hear.

1. <u>What will</u> you say to him tonight?

2. <u>When'll</u> Tony be home?

3. The <u>studen will</u> need paper and pencils for the test.

4. <u>who'll</u> help me carry these bags?

5. <u>Amy'll</u> help you with your homework.

6. After the test, the <u>teacher'll</u> grade our papers.

7. <u>Y'hon'll</u> get the job. He's so qualified.

8. The <u>game'll</u> be over at ten o'clock.

E *Will* vs. *Be Going To*

Examining Meaning and Use

Read the conversations and answer the questions below. Then discuss your answers and read the Meaning and Use Notes to check them.

a. **Waiter:** Our special today is chicken salad.
   Customer: I think I'll have a tuna sandwich instead, please. *quick decision*

b. **Father:** I'm very angry with you.
   Daughter: I'm sorry. I'll never lie to you again. *promise*

c. **Wife:** What time are your parents arriving? *prediction*
   Husband: They'll probably be here by six.

1. In which conversation is the second person making a prediction?

2. In which conversation is the second person making a quick decision?

3. In which conversation is the second person making a promise?

Meaning and Use Notes

> **Predictions with *Will* and *Be Going To***
>
> **1A** Use *will* or *be going to* to make predictions (guesses about the future). You can also use *probably* and other adverbs with *will* and *be going to* to express certainty or uncertainty.
>
> | Will | Be Going To |
> |---|---|
> | Electric cars **will become** popular in the next ten years. | Electric cars **are going to become** popular in the next ten years. |
> | They**'ll** <u>probably</u> **win** the championship. | They**'re** <u>probably</u> **going to win** the championship. |
>
> **1B** With predictions, the meanings of *will* and *be going to* are not exactly the same. Use *be going to* when you are more certain that an event will happen because there is evidence. Do not use *will* in this situation.
>
> She**'s going to have** a baby!
> *She'll have a baby! (INCORRECT)

Quick Decisions vs. Advance Plans

2 In statements with *I, will* and *be going to* have different meanings. *Will* is often used to express a quick decision made at the time of speaking (such as an offer to help). *Be going to*, however, shows that you have thought about something in advance. Do not use *be going to* for quick decisions.

Will *for Quick Decisions*	Be Going To *for Advance Plans*
A: I don't have a fork.	A: Do we have plastic forks for the party?
B: **I'll ask** the waiter to bring you one.	B: No. **I'm going to ask** Lisa to bring some.
A: Someone is at the door.	A: Have you decided to buy the car?
B: **I'll get** it.	B: Yes. **I'm going to get** it tomorrow.

Promises with *Will*

3 In statements with *I, will* is often used to express a promise.

A: Chris, please clean your room.
B: **I'll do** it later, Mom. I promise.

E1 Listening for Meaning and Use ▶ Notes 1A, 1B, 2, 3

Listen to each sentence. Is the speaker making a promise, a prediction, or a quick decision? Check (✓) the correct column.

	PROMISE	PREDICTION	QUICK DECISION
1.		✓	
2.			✓
3.			
4.			✓
5.			
6.	✓		

E2 Contrasting *Be Going To* and *Will*

► Notes 1B, 2

Complete each conversation with the words in parentheses and the correct form of *be going to* or *will*. Use contractions where possible.

Conversation 1

A: _Are you going_ (you/go) to Jake's party?
          1

B: I can't. ~~I'm going to visit~~ (I/visit) my grandmother this weekend.
          2

Conversation 2

A: Did you hear? ~~Maria is going to~~ (Maria/have) a baby in February!
          1   have

B: That's great news!

Conversation 3

A: Oh, there's the doorbell.

B: Don't worry. _I'll answer_ (I/answer) it.
          1

Conversation 4

A: Maria, I have to ask you something important. _will you marry_ (you/marry) me?
          1

B: Yes, of course, _I will_ (I), Luis.
          2

E3 Making Quick Decisions

► Note 2

Complete each conversation with an offer of help. Use *will* and a contraction.

Conversation 1

A: My cat is stuck in the tree again! I'll never get him down.

B: _Don't worry! I'll get him down for you._

Conversation 2

A: I can't open the door. I'm carrying too many groceries.

B: _I'll help you. I'll open the door._

Conversation 3

A: Oh no! I don't have enough money to pay for dinner.

B: _Don't worry I'll pay for you._

Conversation 4

A: I'll never have time to clean this apartment before my mom comes over.

B: Don't worry, I'll do it for you

Conversation 5

A: I lost my math notes and I need them to study for the quiz.

B: Don't worry, I'll lend them to you.

E4 **Making Promises** ► Note 3

Read these situations. Write promises with *will* or *won't*.

1. Tony got bad grades this semester. His parents are angry. What does he promise them?

   I'll study much harder next semester.

2. Derek went away on vacation. He forgot to lock his house. Thieves came in and stole everything. What does he promise himself? I'll lock it nxt tim

   I won't do it again.

3. Pedro forgot his essay. What does he promise his professor?

   I'll bring it to you next class.

4. Dr. Smith is about to give Sara an injection. What does he promise her?

   Don't worry, It won't hurt you.

5. Eve is on the telephone with the manager of the local telephone company. She hasn't paid her bill for three months. What does she promise?

   I'll paid my bills on time.

E5 **Making Predictions** ► Note 1A

Work in small groups. Look at these topics. Make predictions using *be going to* and *will*. Then discuss your predictions with the rest of the class.

1. medicine

   Medical care is going to become more expensive, but more people will have health insurance.

2. space travel

3. war and peace

4. cars and planes

5. education

6. wealth and poverty

Combining Form, Meaning, and Use

F1 Thinking About Meaning and Use

Choose the best answer to complete each conversation. Then discuss your answers in small groups.

1. **A:** _____

   B: I'm getting up early, packing a lunch, and taking a bus to the beach.

   a. What are you doing now?

   b. What are you going to do tomorrow?

2. **A:** I don't need an umbrella. It's not raining.

   B: _____

   a. But it's raining this afternoon.

   b. But it's going to rain this afternoon.

3. **A:** Tomorrow's election is going to be close.

   B: _____

   a. Yes, but I think O'Casey's winning.

   b. Yes, but I think O'Casey will win.

4. **A:** Next Monday is Pat's birthday.

   B: _____

   a. Yes. We're going to have a party for her.

   b. Yes. We'll have a party for her.

5. **A:** This box is very heavy. I can't carry it any longer.

   B: _____

   a. Don't worry. I'm going to carry it.

   b. I'll carry it. You carry the lighter one.

6. **A:** We're going on a Caribbean cruise.

   B: _____

       a. Wow! You're having a great time.

       b. Wow! You're going to have a great time.

7. **A:** Does Lisa know whether she's going to have a boy or a girl?

   B: _____

       a. Yes, the doctor told her. She will have a boy.

       b. Yes, the doctor told her. She's going to have a boy.

8. **A:** Do you think electric cars will become more popular in the future?

   B: _____

       a. Yes, everyone will drive them.

       b. Yes, everyone is driving them.

F2 Editing

Some of these sentences have errors. Find the errors and correct them.

1. Betty <u>is</u> going to college this fall.

2. What she is going to study?

3. She is going to study cooking because she wants to be a chef.

4. Betty studying with some famous chefs next year.

5. Someday maybe Betty is being a famous chef, too.

6. Betty is also going to take some business classes.

7. After these classes she certainly wills know all about restaurant management.

8. Maybe in a few years Betty owns a restaurant.

9. What kind of food her restaurant will serve?

10. I predict it is serving Chinese.

▶ Beyond the Classroom

Searching for Authentic Examples

Find examples of English grammar in everyday life. Look in an English-language newspaper or on the Internet for articles about the future plans of the government or of a famous person. Find five examples of *will, be going to,* and the present continuous as future. Bring the examples to class. Which examples show predictions? advance plans? intentions? Why is *will, be going to,* or the present continuous used in each example? Discuss your findings with your classmates.

Speaking

Follow these steps for making a group presentation about your plans to solve a problem in your school or community.

1. Work with two or three other students outside of class. Think of a problem in your school or community.

2. Discuss the problem as a group. Makes notes about what the problem is, and how to fix it. Use these questions to help you.
   - What is the problem?
   - What are you or others going to do to fix the problem?
   - What results do you predict?

3. Use your notes to prepare your presentation. Be sure to use *be going to,* the present continuous as future, and *will* to talk about your plans and your predictions about the results.

4. Divide the presentation into three or four parts (one for each student in the group). Then present your plan to your classmates. At the end of the presentation, ask your classmates to ask questions and give their opinions about your plan.

   A lot of families in our neighborhood are not following the city's recycling laws. We are going to organize a campaign. First, we will . . .

Future Time Clauses and *If* Clauses

A What Will Happen in the Future?

A1 Before You Read

Discuss these questions.

Do you think about life in the future? What will be different in the future? Will the world be a better or worse place than it is today? Why?

A2 Read

Read this magazine article to find out if your predictions about the future match one expert's predictions.

What Will Happen in the Future?

In the year 2010 we will continue the exploration of the planet Mars. The first interplanetary astronauts won't be humans, however. They will
5 be robots. Experts say these robots will be very different from the robots we usually see in movies. They won't have arms and legs. Instead, they will be like small armored vehicles. They
10 will explore the surface of the planet and they will perform scientific experiments. If the robots find water, humans will travel to Mars and create a colony.

15 **In the year 2015** people will live in "smart" houses. These houses will

Robots of the future probably won't look like this.

use less energy and will be more environmentally friendly than the houses of today. If a room is empty, the lights and TV will go off. When the weather is cold, windows will shut automatically. They will open when the weather is hot. The windows will also change the energy of the sun into electricity. Some people say that smart houses are not going to be very popular because we will prefer our traditional houses. Others say that smart houses will change our way of life completely and everyone will love them.

In the year 2020 it will be possible for ordinary people to travel on supersonic planes such as the Concorde. Today this kind of travel is extremely expensive. However, in the future it is going to be much cheaper. After prices go down, it will be possible for everyone to travel from Tokyo to New York in just a few hours.

In the year 2025 we will build a space station on one of the moons of Jupiter. Some scientists believe that humans will travel into deep space soon after that.

---

armored: covered in metal as protection from damage or attack

colony: a community of people living together in a new place

extremely: very

ordinary: like everyone else, not unusual

supersonic: traveling faster than sound

A3 After You Read

Check (✓) the predictions that the writer makes in the article.

__✓__ 1. The first interplanetary astronauts will not be humans.

_____ 2. It is unlikely that robots will find water on Mars.

_____ 3. Humans will start a colony on Mars in the year 2010.

_____ 4. In 2015 smart houses will use energy from the sun.

_____ 5. People in smart houses will not need electricity.

_____ 6. In the year 2025 we will build a space station on one of the moons of Jupiter.

B Future Time Clauses and *If* Clauses

Examining Form

Read the sentences and complete the tasks below. Then discuss your answers and read the Form charts to check them.

a. I'll see him before I leave.
b. When they graduate, they're going to look for work.
c. We're going to have dessert after we finish dinner.

1. Underline the main clause and circle the dependent clause in each sentence. What form of the verb is used in each main clause?

2. Look at each dependent clause. What is the first word? What form of the verb is used? These are future time clauses.

3. Look at this sentence. What is the first word of the dependent clause? This is an *if* clause.

   If I go to the store, I'll buy the groceries.

4. Look back at the article on page 138. Find two future time clauses and one *if* clause.

FUTURE TIME CLAUSES

FUTURE TIME CLAUSE				MAIN CLAUSE	
	SUBJECT	**VERB**			
Before	I	**go**	to the movies,	**I'm going to do** my homework.	
When	she	**gets**	to work,	she**'ll make** some phone calls.	
After	we	**finish**	dinner,	we**'ll wash** the dishes.	

MAIN CLAUSE		FUTURE TIME CLAUSE			
			SUBJECT	**VERB**	
I'm going to do my homework		**before**	I	**go**	to the movies.
She'll make some phone calls		**when**	she	**gets**	to work.
We'll wash the dishes		**after**	we	**finish**	dinner.

Overview
- A clause is a group of words that has a subject and a verb.
- A main clause can stand alone as a complete sentence.
- A dependent clause cannot stand alone and must be used with a main clause.

Future Time Clauses
- Future time clauses are dependent time clauses. They begin with words such as *before, when, while,* and *after.*
- A future time clause can come before or after the main clause with no change in meaning. If the future time clause comes first, then it is separated from the main clause by a comma.
- Use *will* or *be going to* in the main clause.
- The verb in the future time clause is in the simple present even though it has a future meaning.

⚠ Do not use *be going to* or *will* in the future time clause.

    After I **finish** my work, I'll watch TV.

    * After I will finish my work, I'll watch TV. (INCORRECT)

IF CLAUSES

	IF CLAUSE			(THEN)	MAIN CLAUSE
IF	SUBJECT	VERB		(THEN)	
	you	**exercise**	every day,		you**'ll feel** better.
If	it	**rains**	tomorrow,	(then)	they**'ll cancel** the picnic.
	we	**don't score**	soon,		we**'re going to lose** the game.

MAIN CLAUSE		IF CLAUSE		
	IF	SUBJECT	VERB	
You**'ll feel** better		you	**exercise**	every day.
They**'ll cancel** the picnic	if	it	**rains**	tomorrow.
We**'re going to lose** the game		we	**don't score**	soon.

(Continued on page 142)

If Clauses

- *If* clauses are dependent clauses. They must be used with a main clause.
- An *if* clause can come before or after the main clause with no change in meaning. When the *if* clause comes first, it is separated from the main clause by a comma.
- When the *if* clause comes first, *then* can be added before the main clause with no change in meaning.
- Use *will* or *be going to* in the main clause.
- The verb in the *if* clause is in the simple present even though it has a future meaning.
- ⚠ Do not use *be going to* or *will* in the *if* clause.

    If I **finish** my work, I'll watch TV.

    * If I'll finish my work, I'll watch TV. (INCORRECT)

B1 Listening for Form

🎧 Listen to these sentences. Write the verb forms you hear.

1. When I _____ *see* _____ Elena, I _'ll give_ _____ her the message.

2. We'_ll need_ _____ more time if the test _____ *is* _____ very difficult.

3. Marcus and Maria _will go_ _____ to Budapest after they _visite_ _____ Prague.

4. She _'ll call_ _____ us when she _____ *gets* _____ here.

5. You _'ll meet_ _____ him if you _____ *go* _____ to the party.

6. If Matt _____ *gets* _____ a loan from the bank, he _'ll buy_ _____ a new car.

B2 Building Sentences

Build five logical sentences with future time clauses and *if* clauses. Use a clause from each column. Use the correct form of the verbs in parentheses. Punctuate your sentences correctly.

After Megan finishes class, she'll have lunch.

after Megan (finish) class	we (get) a lot of money
before she (leave) the house	she (have) lunch
if we (win) the prize	you (pass) the test
if you (study) hard	she (call) you
when we (get) to the movies	we (save) you a seat

A. Complete each sentence with a future time clause or a main clause. Use the words and phrases in parentheses and the correct punctuation.

1. When I get a job, I'll buy a car.   (I/buy/a car)

2. After she graduates (after/she/graduate) she's going to move to L.A.

3. After we save some money we'll look for (we/look/for a house) a house.

4. they'll visit (they/visit/the Eiffel Tower) before they leave Paris.

B. Complete each sentence with an *if* clause or a main clause. Use the words and phrases in parentheses and the correct punctuation.

1. We'll take her out to dinner if she visits.   (if/she/visit)

2. I'll call (I/call) if I hear any news.

3. If I feel better I'll go to work. (I/go/to work)

4. If you don't study (if/you/not/study) you won't do well on the test.

Complete this e-mail with the correct form of the verb in parentheses.

Emily,

We're planning a surprise party for Dan's birthday. Here are the plans.

Lauren _will bring_ (bring) me their house key after Dan _leaves_ (leave)
                1   2

for work on Friday. I _ll decorate_ (decorate) before I _go_ (go) to class.
                        3   4

I ordered a cake from the bakery. Stefan _will get_ (get) it when he
                                           5

goes (go) shopping on Friday afternoon. We need your help. If Dan
 6

comes (come) home right after work, we _won't be_ (not/be) ready.
 7   8

Will you ask him to drive you home after work? If you _ask_ (ask) him to
                                                        9

take you home, he _won't be_ (not/ be) suspicious. Then, when everyone
                    10

_is_ (be) here, I _ll call_ (call) you on your cell phone.
 11   12

Luisa

C Using Future Time Clauses for Events in Sequence

Examining Meaning and Use

Read the sentences and complete the task below. Then discuss your answers and read the Meaning and Use Notes to check them.

> **a.** We'll give you the information when we get the results.
> **b.** Before you take the test, the teacher will review the homework.
> **c.** He'll need help after he comes home from the hospital.

Look at each sentence. Underline the event that happens first. Which word or words in each sentence tell you the order of the events?

Meaning and Use Notes

> **Future Events in Sequence**
>
> **1** Future time clauses show the time relationship between two events or situations in a sentence. When a time clause begins with *when* or *after*, the event in the time clause happens first. When a time clause begins with *before*, the event in the time clause happens second.
>
> | First Event | Second Event |
> |---|---|
> | **When I get home,** | I'll call you. |
> | **After they get married,** | they're going to move to California. |
> | I'm going to water the plants | **before I go on vacation.** |

C1 Listening for Meaning and Use ► Note 1

🎧 Listen to each sentence. Which event happens first and which happens second? Write *1* next to the first event and *2* next to the second.

1. __1__ I look for a job. ~~before~~ __2__ I graduate.

2. __2__ He gets here. __1__ We make dinner.

3. __2__ We go to the park. *after* __1__ We go to the museum.

4. __2__ I call you. *after* __1__ They leave.

5. __2__ I clean the house. __1__ I go shopping.
   before.

C2 **Talking About Two Future Events** ► Note 1

A. Complete these sentences with future time clauses or main clauses.

1. _When I finish school_, my family will be happy.

2. After I finish this English class, _I'll take business classes._

3. _After spring classes finish_, I'll take a vacation.

4. I'll buy a new car _After I save some money._

5. _After I finish ESL classes_, I'll speak English.

6. I'll be happy _After I move to my new house._

B. Work with a partner. In your notebook, write two main clauses and two future time clauses. Have your partner complete each one.

I'll call you _____

When my friend visits me, _____

C3 **Describing Future Events in Sequence** ► Note 1

Think about your day tomorrow. Write two sentences for each part of the day. Use future time clauses with *before, when,* and *after.*

1. (tomorrow morning)

   I'll get up when my alarm rings.

   I'll take a shower.

2. (tomorrow afternoon)

   I'll do my homework after dinner.

3. (tomorrow evening)

   I'll watch TV after I wash the dishes.

4. (tomorrow night)

   Before I go to bed I'll read a good book.

D Expressing Future Possibility with *If* Clauses

Examining Meaning and Use

Read the sentences and complete the tasks below. Then discuss your answers and read the Meaning and Use Notes to check them.

1a. If you take some aspirin, you'll feel better.
1b. I'll take you out to dinner if you help me with the housework.

2a. If Ben leaves, call me.
2b. When Ben leaves, call me.

1. Look at 1a and 1b. Underline the *if* clauses. Circle the main clauses. Which clause in each sentence describes a possible situation? Which clause in each sentence describes a possible result of that situation?

2. Look at 1a and 1b again. Which sentence gives advice? Which sentence makes a promise?

3. Look at 2a and 2b. In which sentence is it more certain that Ben will leave?

Meaning and Use Notes

> **Cause-and-Effect Relationships**
>
> **1** Sentences with an *if* clause show a cause-and-effect relationship. The *if* clause introduces a possible situation (the cause). The main clause talks about the possible result (the effect) of that situation. The cause and effect can come in either order.
>
> | If *Clause (Cause)* | Main Clause *(Effect)* |
> |---|---|
> | **If she gets that job,** | her salary will increase. |
> | **If you press the red button,** | the elevator will stop. |
>
> | Main Clause *(Effect)* | If *Clause (Cause)* |
> |---|---|
> | Her salary will increase | **if she gets that job.** |
> | The elevator will stop | **if you press the red button.** |

2 Sentences with an *if* clause and a main clause with *be going to* or *will* have several common uses:

Giving Advice:	If you rest now, you'll feel better later.
Giving a Warning:	If you don't tell the truth, you're going to be sorry.
Making a Promise:	If you elect me, I won't raise taxes.
Making a Prediction:	If he moves to the city, he won't be happy.

Possibility vs. Certainty

3 Use an *if* clause if you think something is possible but you are not sure it will happen. Use a future time clause with *when* if you are certain something will happen.

If *Clause (Possible)*	Future Time Clause *(Certain)*
If it goes on sale, I'll buy it.	**When it goes on sale,** I'll buy it.
I'll visit the Taj Mahal **if I go to India.**	I'll visit the Taj Mahal **when I go to India.**

D1 Listening for Meaning and Use ▶ Note 3

Listen to each conversation. Does the second speaker think the situation is possible or certain? Check (✓) the correct column.

	SITUATION	POSSIBLE	CERTAIN
1.	She and Amy will see a movie.	✓	
2.	He will go to the store.		
3.	It will snow this weekend.		
4.	He will go to Mexico.		
5.	Mark will ask Celia to marry him.		
6.	Jake will rent the apartment.		

D2 Giving Warnings

▶ Notes 1, 2

Complete each warning with an *if* clause or a main clause.

1. If you don't stop at a red light, _you'll get a ticket_ .

2. You'll burn your hand _If you touch the stove_.

3. _They turn off the electricity_ if you don't pay your electric bill.

4. If you go swimming in cold weather, _you'll get sick._ .

5. _You'll be_ _____ if you don't eat breakfast.

6. _You'll be very sleepy_ if you stay up all night.

7. You'll lose your job _if you don't arrive on time_.

8. _If you don't watch your steps_ , you'll break your leg.

D3 Giving Advice

▶ Notes 1, 2

Write two pieces of advice for the person in each situation. Each piece of advice should include an *if* clause and a main clause.

1. Your friend is always late for school.

   a. _If you leave home on time, you won't be late for school._

   b. _If you're always late for class, you'll miss important information._

2. Your brother wants to go to a good university.

   a. _You'll have to save money if you want to go to a good university._

   b. _If you want to go to a good university, you'll have to get good grades._

3. Your sister doesn't get along with a co-worker.

   a. _If you ask her what the problem is,_

   b. _you'll understand her._

4. Your cousin wants to move to a new apartment, but he doesn't have much money.

   a. _If you get a extra job, you'll have enough_

   b. _money to get a new apartment._

Work with a partner. Read these situations. Take turns making promises. Each promise should include an *if* clause and a main clause. Switch roles after each situation.

1. **Student A:** You are a student. You need help with your English homework.
   Student B: You are the student's best friend.

   A: If you help me with my English homework, I'll help you with your math.
   B: I'll help you with your homework if you let me ride your motorcycle.

2. **Student A:** You are a teenager. You want to borrow the family car.
   Student B: You are the teenager's parent.

3. **Student A:** You are a driver. You were speeding.
   Student B: You are a police officer.

4. **Student A:** You are an employee. You are often late for work.
   Student B: You are the employee's boss.

Look at the picture. Write predictions about what will happen. Include an *if* clause and a main clause in each prediction.

If the man trips over the telephone cord, he'll fall.

Combining Form, Meaning, and Use

E1 Thinking About Meaning and Use

Read each sentence and the statements that follow. Check (✓) the statement that has the same meaning. Then discuss your answers in small groups.

1. After the children go to bed, we'll leave.

    _____ **a.** We'll leave, and then the children will go to bed.

    __✓__ **b.** The children will go to bed, and then we'll leave.

2. He'll come and get us when the program starts.

    __✓__ **a.** The program will start, and then he'll come and get us.

    _____ **b.** He'll come and get us, and then the program will start.

3. Before you graduate, you'll need another math course.

    __✓__ **a.** You can't graduate without another math course.

    _____ **b.** You'll graduate, and then you'll take another math course.

4. He'll leave before I leave.

    _____ **a.** I'll leave when he leaves.

    _____ **b.** He'll leave, and then I'll leave.

5. He'll be happy if he gets the job.

    _____ **a.** He'll get the job, and then he'll be happy.

    __✓__ **b.** It's possible that he'll get the job. If he does, he'll be happy.

6. We're going to buy a house when we get married.

    __✓__ **a.** We feel certain that we'll buy a house after we marry.

    _____ **b.** We don't feel certain that we'll get married and buy a house.

7. If the store is open, I'll buy some milk.

_____ **a.** The store will be open, so I'll buy some milk.

__✓__ **b.** Maybe the store will be open, and I'll buy some milk.

8. I'll help you when I finish making lunch.

__✓__ **a.** I'll make lunch. Then I'll help you.

_____ **b.** I'll help you. At the same time, I'll make lunch.

9. She'll cook dinner when her husband comes home.

__✓__ **a.** Dinner will not be ready when he arrives.

_____ **b.** Dinner will be ready when he arrives.

10. I'll see Ben if I go to the party.

__✓__ **a.** I'm not certain that I'm going to the party.

_____ **b.** Ben isn't certain that he's going to the party.

E2 **Editing**

Some of these sentences have errors. Find the errors and correct them. There may be more than one error in some sentences.

1. When I ~~will~~ see Debbie, I'll give her the book.

2. If I ~~won't~~ don't feel better soon, I'll go to the doctor.

3. If I get an A on the final, then I'll get an A for the course.

4. I'm going to check the prices on-line before I ~~'m going to~~ buy a camera.

5. We won't have time to see a movie after we go shopping.

6. He's going to drive to Dallas if the weather ~~will~~ improve**s**.

7. When I ~~'ll~~ get my paycheck, I'll pay my bills.

8. They**'ll** cancel the picnic if it ~~will~~ rain**s** tomorrow.

9. When the phone ~~is going to~~ ring**s**, I'll answer it.

10. She'll be rich if she wins the lottery.

▶ Beyond the Classroom

Searching for Authentic Examples

Find examples of grammar in everyday life. Look for advertisements in an English-language newspaper or magazine, or on the Internet. Find five sentences with *if* clauses and bring them to class. What does each *if* clause express? Is it advice? a warning? a promise? a prediction? Discuss your findings with your classmates.

Writing

Imagine you are running for election as mayor of your town or city. Follow these steps to write a campaign flyer.

1. Work with a partner. Think about the topic. Brainstorm the changes that you will make as mayor.

2. Makes notes about what you want to say. Use these questions to help you.
   - What problems does your city have?
   - How will you solve these problems if the people elect you?
   - What will happen when you solve these problems?

3. Write a first draft. Use future time clauses and *if* clauses to make predictions, promises, and warnings.

4. Read your work carefully and circle grammar, spelling, and punctuation errors. Work with your partner to decide how to fix your errors and improve the content.

5. Rewrite your draft.
   - When I become mayor, I will work hard to improve our city.
   - If you elect me, I will not raise taxes.

Modals

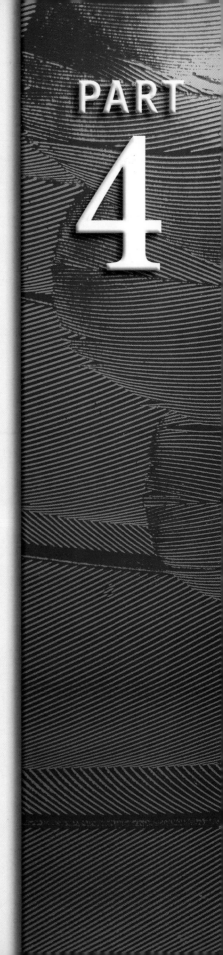

Modals of Ability and Possibility

A | A Real-Life Hero

Discuss these questions.

What is a hero? Can an ordinary person be a hero? Do you know any heroes?

Read this magazine article to find out why a man who played a hero in the movies is a real-life hero today.

▌▌▌ feature story

A Real-Life Hero

Reeve as Superman

Everyone knows Superman. He's a comic book hero. He <u>can do</u> things that ordinary people can't do. And most people know Christopher Reeve. He's the
5 actor who played Superman in four movies. As Superman, Reeve <u>could fly</u>. He could see through walls. He had the strength of one hundred men, and his enemies could not defeat him. These
10 movies were very popular, and for most people Christopher Reeve was Superman—until May 26, 1995.

On that day Reeve was in a horse-jumping competition. His horse couldn't
15 jump over a hurdle, and Reeve fell. He injured his spinal cord very badly. Now he is paralyzed—he is not able to move any part of his body below his neck. He cannot write, walk, or even feed
20 himself. A machine helps him breathe. He is able to talk, but his voice is often difficult to understand.

What kind of life does Reeve have after this terrible accident? Does he

25 spend his time feeling sorry for himself? No. In fact, he's still a very busy man. He still acts in films and directs them. Most importantly, he makes speeches and raises money for the study of spinal cord 30 injuries. He has also started a research center.

Reeve today

Reeve has brought hope to other people who are paralyzed. He speaks to people all over the country with similar 35 injuries. He tells them that they can still have useful lives, and he explains his idea of what makes a hero. According to Reeve, a hero is an ordinary person who can find the strength to continue even 40 with serious problems.

Christopher Reeve has made some progress with special exercise. He has recovered some feeling in his left leg and parts of his left arm. Although doctors 45 think that he will always be paralyzed, Christopher Reeve still has hope for the future. Researchers may find a cure for spinal cord injuries. Reeve believes that he might even walk again. And who knows? For 50 this real-life hero, nothing is impossible.

---

competition: a contest or an athletic event
cure: something that makes a sick person healthy
defeat: to beat someone in a fight or battle
enemy: a person who hates or wants to hurt somebody

hurdle: a fence or wall that horses jump over in a race
spinal cord: a system of nerves in the back that connects the brain to other parts of the body

A3 After You Read

Write *T* for true or *F* for false for each statement.

__F__ **1.** Christopher Reeve was not famous before his accident.

_____ **2.** Christopher Reeve is still a busy man.

_____ **3.** Christopher Reeve gives hope to people with spinal cord injuries.

_____ **4.** The doctors think Christopher Reeve will walk again.

_____ **5.** Christopher Reeve doesn't believe that ordinary people can be heroes.

_____ **6.** Christopher Reeve feels positive about the future.

B Modals of Ability: *Can* and *Could*; *Be Able To*

Examining Form

Look back at the article on page 156 and complete the tasks below. Then discuss your answers and read the Form charts to check them.

1. Look at the underlined examples of *can* + verb and *could* + verb. What form of the verb follows *can* and *could*?

2. Find the negative forms of *can* + verb and *could* + verb in the first paragraph. What is unusual about the negative form of *can* + verb? What are the contracted negative forms of *can* and *could*?

CAN FOR PRESENT AND FUTURE ABILITY

Affirmative Statements

SUBJECT	MODAL	BASE FORM OF VERB	
I		**play**	the piano.
He	**can**		
They		**work**	tomorrow.

Negative Statements

SUBJECT	MODAL + *NOT*	BASE FORM OF VERB	
I		**play**	the piano.
He	**cannot** **can't**		
They		**work**	tomorrow.

Yes/No Questions

MODAL	SUBJECT	BASE FORM OF VERB	
	you	**play**	the piano?
Can	he		
	they	**work**	tomorrow?

Short Answers

YES	SUBJECT	MODAL	NO	SUBJECT	MODAL + *NOT*
	I			I	
Yes,	he	**can.**	**No,**	he	**can't.**
	they			they	

Information Questions

WH- WORD	MODAL	SUBJECT	BASE FORM OF VERB	
What	**can**	you	**play**?	
How long		he	**work**	tomorrow?

WH- WORD (SUBJECT)	MODAL		BASE FORM OF VERB	
Who	**can**		**work**	tomorrow?
What			**fly**?	

- *Can* is a modal. Like all modals, it is followed by the base form of a verb and has the same form for all subjects.
- The negative form of *can* is *cannot*. Notice that *cannot* is written as one word.
- It is often difficult to hear the difference between *can* and *can't* because the final *t* in *can't* is not clearly pronounced. In sentences with *can* + verb, the vowel sound in *can* is very short and the stress is on the verb that follows *can:* I/kən/gö. In sentences with *can't* + verb, the stress is on *can't* and the *a* is pronounced like the *a* in *ant*: I/kæn/gö.

COULD FOR PAST ABILITY

Affirmative Statements

SUBJECT	MODAL	BASE FORM OF VERB	
I			
He	**could**	**read**	in kindergarten.
They			

Negative Statements

SUBJECT	MODAL + *NOT*	BASE FORM OF VERB	
I			
He	**could not** **couldn't**	**read**	in kindergarten.
They			

Yes/No Questions

MODAL	SUBJECT	BASE FORM OF VERB	
Could	you	**read**	in kindergarten?

Short Answers

YES	SUBJECT	MODAL		NO	SUBJECT	MODAL + *NOT*
Yes,	I	**could.**		**No**	I	**couldn't.**

(Continued on page 160)

Information Questions

WH- WORD	MODAL	SUBJECT	BASE FORM OF VERB	
What	**could**	she	**read**	in kindergarten?

WH- WORD (SUBJECT)	MODAL		BASE FORM OF VERB	
Who	**could**		**read**	in kindergarten?

- *Could* is a modal. Like all modals, it is followed by the base form of a verb and has the same form for all subjects.

BE ABLE TO FOR PAST, PRESENT, AND FUTURE ABILITY

Affirmative Statements

SUBJECT	BE ABLE TO	BASE FORM OF VERB	
	was able to		yesterday.
He	**is able to**	**work**	today.
	will be able to		tomorrow.

Negative Statements

SUBJECT	BE + NOT + ABLE TO	BASE FORM OF VERB	
	was not able to		yesterday.
He	**is not able to**	**work**	today.
	will not be able to		tomorrow.

- *Be able to* is not a modal, but it has the same meaning as *can* and *could*. The verb *be* in *be able to* changes form and agrees with the subject.
- See Appendix 16 for contractions with *be* and *will*.

B1 Listening for Form

Listen to this paragraph. Write *can* or *can't*.

Michael is blind. He ___can't___ see. He _____ do amazing things, however. He
₁   ₂

lives in Chicago, and he _____ walk around the city alone. Of course, he _____
₃   ₄

read the street signs, so sometimes he asks for help. After he has been somewhere with a

friend, he _____ go there again by himself. Michael is good at sports, too. He's the best
₅

player on his bowling team, even though he _____ see the bowling pins.
₆

B2 Building Sentences with *Can* and *Can't*

Build three logical sentences with *can* and three logical sentences with *can't*. Use a word from each column. Punctuate your sentences correctly.

People can climb trees.

people		climb trees
fish	can	bark
	can't	
dogs		swim

B3 Forming Statements and Questions with *Can* and *Could*

In your notebook, write a statement and a question for each set of words and phrases. Punctuate your sentences correctly.

1. Emily/party/can/our/come/to

   Emily can come to our party.
   Can Emily come to our party?

2. them/airport/could/we/the/take/to

   We could take them to the air port
   Could we take them to the airport.

3. his/languages/can/parents/speak/several

4. sister/your/can/Mandarin/speak

5. problem/us/can/she/this/with/help

B4 Completing Conversations with *Be Able To*

Complete these conversations with the words in parentheses and the correct form of *be able to*. Use contractions where possible.

1. **A:** ___Were___ you ___able to finish___ (finish) the test yesterday?
   1   2

   B: No, __I wasn't able to__ (not), but I __was able to__ (do) 45 out of
              3   4

   the 50 questions.

2. **A:** Did David help you clean the attic?

   B: No, he __wasn't able to come.__ (not/come) on Saturday. But I think he
                     1

   __will be able to__ (help) me this weekend.
        2

3. **A:** __Was__ Susan __able to__ (practice) the piano at college last year?
            1   2

   B: Well, not in the dorm, but she __was able to__ (play) at the Student Center.
                                              3

4. **A:** __Are__ you __able to__ (call) me later?
            1   2

   B: No. I'm busy tonight, but I __'ll be able to__ (see) you tomorrow.
                                           3

Past, Present, and Future Ability

Examining Meaning and Use

Read the sentences and answer the questions below. Then discuss your answers and read the Meaning and Use Notes to check them.

  a. Carl can type 40 words a minute.
  b. Last year Carl could type 20 words a minute.
  c. When Carl's typing class ends, he will be able to type 60 words a minute.

1. Which sentence talks about an ability that Carl has at the present time?

2. Which sentence talks about an ability Carl doesn't have yet?

3. Which sentence talks about an ability Carl had in the past?

Meaning and Use Notes

Present Ability with *Can*

1A *Can* is used to talk about an ability in the present.

The baby **can walk,** but she **can't talk** yet.
Strong winds **can cause** a lot of damage.

1B *Be able to* also describes an ability in the present, but *can* is more commonly used.

Less Common   *More Common*
He **is able to** speak French and Arabic.   He **can speak** French and Arabic.

Future Ability with *Be Able To* and *Can*

2A Use *will be able to* to talk about a skill or other ability that you don't have yet, but will have in the future. Do not use *can* to describe an ability that you will have only in the future.

After I complete this class, **I'll be able to type** 60 words a minute.
*After I complete this class, I can type 60 words a minute. (INCORRECT)
I will be able to see better after I get new glasses.
*I can see better after I get new glasses. (INCORRECT)

2B Use *will be able to* or *can* to express ability that relates to decisions and arrangements for the future.

She $\begin{Bmatrix} \textbf{'ll be able to} \\ \textbf{can} \end{Bmatrix}$ **meet** you at the airport at 3:00.

I'm busy now, but I $\begin{Bmatrix} \textbf{'ll be able to} \\ \textbf{can} \end{Bmatrix}$ **help** you in ten minutes.

Past Ability with *Could* and *Be Able To*

3A Use *could* or *was/were able to* to talk about an ability that existed for a long period of time in the past.

Long Period of Time

When I was young, I $\begin{Bmatrix} \textbf{was able to} \\ \textbf{could} \end{Bmatrix}$ **eat** dessert every night and I didn't gain weight.

3B In affirmative statements with action verbs, do not use *could* to talk about an ability related to a single event. Use only *was/were able to*.

Single Event with Action Verb (Affirmative)
Yesterday I **was able to finish** my homework quickly.
*Yesterday I could finish my homework quickly. (INCORRECT)

3C In affirmative statements with certain stative verbs such as *see, hear, feel, taste, understand,* and *remember,* use *could* or *was/were able to* to talk about ability related to a single event in the past.

Single Event with Stative Verb (Affirmative)

Last night the sky was clear and we $\begin{Bmatrix} \textbf{were able to} \\ \textbf{could} \end{Bmatrix}$ **see** for miles.

3D In negative statements, use *couldn't* or *wasn't/weren't able to* for both ability during single events and ability over a long period of time.

Single Event (Negative)

Yesterday I $\begin{Bmatrix} \textbf{wasn't able to} \\ \textbf{couldn't} \end{Bmatrix}$ **finish** my homework quickly.

Long Period of Time

When I was younger, I $\begin{Bmatrix} \textbf{wasn't able to} \\ \textbf{couldn't} \end{Bmatrix}$ **finish** my homework quickly.

C1 Listening for Meaning and Use

▶ Notes 1–3

🎧 **Listen to each speaker. Choose the correct response.**

1. **a.** OK, let's go today.
   (b.) OK, we'll go tomorrow.

2. **a.** No, they can't. It's raining.
   b. Why not?

3. **a.** Were they very high?
   b. How disappointing!

4. **a.** Well, at least she tries.
   b. Of course she can. Her dad's a coach.

5. **a.** So what did they do?
   b. When did they learn?

6. **a.** Is she able to walk now?
   b. Will she be able to walk tomorrow?

C2 Talking About Future Abilities

▶ Note 2A

Complete the sentences with *will/won't* + *be able to*. Use your own ideas.

1. Next year <u>I'll be able to drive.</u>

2. In 20 years people _____

3. In 50 years doctors _____

4. By 2020 scientists _____

5. In 10 years I _____

6. In 100 years humans _____

C3 Distinguishing Between Can and Be Able To

▶ Notes 2A, 2B

In your notebook, rewrite these sentences with *can* where possible.

1. The teacher will be able to help you with your homework this afternoon.
   The teacher can help you with your homework this afternoon.

2. Paul will be able to drive us to school tomorrow morning.

3. Larry will be able to get a job when he learns how to use a computer.

4. Will you be able to swim after you finish this swimming class?

5. The doctor will be able to see you at three o'clock this afternoon.

6. He will be able to walk again after the operation.

C4 Talking About Past Abilities

A. Work with a partner. Look at the topics below, and think about how people lived fifty years ago. Take turns making sentences with *could(n't)* and *was/were (not) able to.*

education	food	housing	relationships
energy	health	leisure time	transportation

A: *Fifty years ago many people weren't able to go to college.*
B: *Fifty years ago you could buy a house for ten thousand dollars.*

B. Share your ideas with your classmates.

C5 Comparing Long Periods of Time and Single Events

A. In your notebook, rewrite these sentences with *could* or *couldn't* where possible. Do not change the meaning.

1. For many years, we were able to take long vacations.

   For many years, we could take long vacations.

2. They were able to get tickets for the play this morning.

3. Before he hurt his knee, he was able to run five miles a day.

4. Even as a young child, she was able to swim well.

5. We weren't able to get to the concert on time last night.

6. Were you able to see the fireworks from your window the other night?

7. Matt wasn't able to find his keys this morning.

8. I was able to park the car in front of the restaurant this morning.

B. Look back at the sentences in part A. Which sentences cannot be rewritten? Why?

Vocabulary Notes

Know How To

You can use *know how to* instead of *can* to talk about a skill (a particular ability that you develop through training or practice).

KNOW HOW TO	**CAN**
They **know how to** speak Portuguese.	They **can** speak Portuguese.
She **doesn't know how** to drive a car.	She **can't** drive a car.

We do not use *know how to* to talk about abilities that do not require training or practice. We use *can* instead.

CAN

Hurricanes **can** cause damage.
*Hurricanes know how to cause damage. (INCORRECT)
The doctor **can** see you now.
*The doctor knows how to see you now. (INCORRECT)

C6 Talking About Skills

A. Ask your classmates questions to find out who has the skills on the list. Ask four questions with *can* and four questions with *know how to*.

1. do the tango (or other dance)

   Can you do the tango? OR *Do you know how to do the tango?*

2. change a tire

3. use a computer

4. sew on a button

5. play the guitar (or other instrument)

6. play baseball

7. speak French

8. drive a motorcycle

B. Work in small groups. Talk about your classmates' abilities. Use *can* and *know how to*.

Carlos can do the tango, but Mei Ling can't. OR *Carlos knows how to do the tango, but Mei Ling doesn't.*

Modals of Future Possibility

Examining Form

Read the sentences and complete the tasks below. Then discuss your answers and read the Form charts to check them.

a. He might walk again.
b. He has the strength of one hundred men.
c. Researchers may find a cure.

1. Which sentences contain modals? Underline them. Which sentence contains a verb in the simple present?

2. Change all the sentences to negative statements. How are the negative statements with modals different from the negative statement in the simple present?

Affirmative Statements			
SUBJECT	MODAL	BASE FORM OF VERB	
I			
You	**might** **may** **could** **will**	**leave**	tomorrow.
He			
They			

Negative Statements			
SUBJECT	MODAL + *NOT*	BASE FORM OF VERB	
I			
You	**might not** **may not** **won't**	**leave**	tomorrow.
He			
They			

Yes/No Questions
FUTURE FORM
Are you going to leave next weekend?
Will you leave next weekend?
Are you leaving next weekend?

Short Answers	
AFFIRMATIVE	NEGATIVE
I **may.**	I **may not.**
I **might.**	I **might not.**
I **could.**	I **may not.** / I **might not.**

(Continued on page 168)

- *Could not (couldn't)* is not usually used to express future possibility.
- *May not* and *might not* are not contracted in American English.
- *Yes/No* questions about future possibility are not usually formed with *may, might,* or *could.* Instead, they are formed with *be going to, will,* or the present continuous as future. You can use *may, might,* or *could* in short answers.
- Use modal + *be* in short answers to questions with *be.*
  - A: Will you **be** home next weekend?
  - B: I **might be.**
- Information questions about future possibility are also usually asked with future forms. You can answer with *may, might,* or *could.*

  A: When are you leaving?   A: When is he going to call?
  B: I'm not sure. **I may leave** next weekend.   B: He **might call** today.

D1) Listening for Form

Listen to these conversations. Write the correct form of the modals you hear.

1. **A:** What will you do when you finish college?

   B: I ___might___ look for a job, or I _____ go to graduate school instead.
   (1)   (2)

2. **A:** The traffic is moving very slowly. We won't get to the theater on time.

   B: We _____. We still have plenty of time.
   (1)

3. **A:** When is the package arriving?

   B: It _____ be here tomorrow, or it _____ arrive until the next day.
   (1)   (2)

4. **A:** Will there be many people at the meeting?

   B: I don't know. There _____ be just a few of us.
   (1)

5. **A:** What do you think? Is it going to snow tonight?

   B: Well, according to the weather report, there _____ be a lot of snow, but
   (1)

   the storm _____ hit us at all.
   (2)

A. Form affirmative statements from these words and phrases. Punctuate your sentences correctly.

1. fail/the/I/might/test

   <u>I might fail the test.</u>

2. game/you/win/next/could/the/Saturday

   _____

3. might/Bob and Carol/married/get/year/next

   _____

4. rain/could/tomorrow/it

   _____

5. tonight/cook/Sara/dinner/will

   _____

6. on/we/go/may/Sunday/beach/the/to

   _____

7. will/Yuji/at six o'clock/come

   _____

8. have/Kim and Josh/a/party/might

   _____

9. Lynn/graduate/could/next semester

   _____

10. stay/may/home/Victor/next weekend

    _____

B. In your notebook, rewrite the sentences as negative statements. Which three sentences cannot be made negative? Why? Discuss your answers with a partner.

   I might not fail the test.

E Future Possibility

Examining Meaning and Use

Read the sentences and answer the questions below. Then discuss your answers and read the Meaning and Use Notes to check them.

- **a.** Ana could leave tomorrow, or she could leave today.
- **b.** Ana will leave tomorrow. She's ready to go.
- **c.** Ana may leave tomorrow. She's ready to go, but it depends on the weather.
- **d.** Maybe Ana will leave tomorrow. I'm not certain.
- **e.** Ana might leave tomorrow. I'm not sure.

Which sentence is the most certain? Which sentences are less certain?

Meaning and Use Notes

> ### Expressing Future Possibility with *Could, Might,* and *May*
>
> **1A** *Could, might (not),* and *may (not)* express possibility about the future. *Could* and *might* sometimes express more uncertainty than *may.*
>
> I **could get** an A or a B in the course. It depends on my final paper.
> I **may take** history next semester. It seems like a good idea.
>
> ---
>
> **1B** You can talk about future possibility and future ability together with *might/may (not) + be able to.* You cannot use *might/may (not) + can.*
>
> It's already April, but I **might be able to go** skiing one more time.
>
> If I learn to speak Portuguese, I **may be able to get** a job in Brazil.
>
> *If I learn to speak Portuguese, I may can get a job in Brazil. (INCORRECT)
>
> ---
>
> **1C** Do not confuse *may be* and *maybe. May be* is the modal *may* and the verb *be. Maybe* is an adverb. It comes at the beginning of a sentence, and it is written as one word. *Maybe* can be used with *will* to express future possibility.
>
> May be *(Modal + Be)*   Maybe *(Adverb)*
> We **may be** away next week. = **Maybe** we'll be away next week.

1D Use *will* in *Yes/No* questions about future possibility. You can use *might* but it will sound overly formal. Do not use *may*.

Will	Might/May
Will he come home soon?	**Might** he come home soon? (OVERLY FORMAL)
	*May he come home soon? (INCORRECT)

Expressing Strong Certainty with *Will*

2 Use *will* when you are certain about something. If you are not certain, you can weaken *will* by adding the adverbs *probably*, *maybe*, and *perhaps*.

Certain	*Not Certain*
They**'ll move** in the summer.	They**'ll probably move** in the summer.
She**'ll find** a new job.	**Maybe she'll find** a new job.

E1 **Listening for Meaning and Use**　　　▶ **Notes 1A, 1B, 2**

🎧 Listen to the conversation. Check (✓) the places that Mark and Dan are definitely going to see on their trip to Florida. Put a question mark (?) next to the places that they aren't sure about.

✓ **1.** Disney World　　　____ **4.** Miami Beach

____ **2.** Epcot Center　　　____ **5.** the Everglades

____ **3.** Cape Canaveral　　____ **6.** Key West

The Colony Hotel, Miami Beach

Complete this conversation by choosing the appropriate word or phrase in parentheses.

A: So what's your daughter Lisa going to do this summer?

B: She's not sure, but she (could / **'ll**) probably work for an architect. What's your son
   1

   going to do? (Will / May) he have the same job as last summer?
   2

A: He isn't sure. He (might / 'll) work in a movie theater again. But there aren't
   3

   many jobs available, so he (couldn't / might not) find one.
   4

B: They (can / might) be able to give him a job at my office. I'll speak to my boss.
   5

   (Maybe / May be) there will be an opening.
   6

A: Oh, thank you! That (maybe / may be) a better way for him to spend the summer.
   7

   I (can / 'll) probably be able to convince him to apply.
   8

Rewrite each sentence in your notebook. If the sentence uses *maybe,*
rewrite it with *may be.* If it uses *may be,* rewrite it with *maybe.* Make all
other necessary changes.

1. Lee's family may be in town next week.

   Maybe Lee's family will be in town next week.

2. Maybe the weather will be better on the weekend.

3. Maybe we'll be able to get tickets to the baseball game.

4. This may be an exciting game.

5. Maybe they won't be home this evening.

6. The final exam may not be very difficult.

7. He may be stuck in traffic.

8. Maybe they'll be able to help us clean the attic.

A. Use your imagination to complete these conversations. Use a modal of future possibility and a verb.

Conversation 1

A: What are your roommates going to do tonight?

B: I don't know. They <u>might go to the movies</u> , but they
₁
<u>may stay home and watch the game on TV</u> .
₂

Conversation 2

A: Can you come to Europe with us this summer?

B: I don't have much money, but I _____.
₁

Conversation 3

A: Tomorrow's Monday again! I don't want to go to school!

B: _____. Then we won't have to go
₁
to school.

Conversation 4

A: What are we having for dinner tonight?

B: We have a couple of choices. We _____, or we
₁
_____.
₂

Conversation 5

A: Where will you go on your next vacation?

B: I'm not sure. _____.
₂

B. With a partner, write two more short conversations about these situations. Use *could, might (not), may (not), maybe, will, won't,* or *be able to.*

A student asks a teacher about finishing a paper late.
A reporter asks an athlete about the next Olympics.

Combining Form, Meaning, and Use

F1 Thinking About Meaning and Use

Choose the best answer to complete each conversation. Then discuss your answers in small groups.

1. **A:** At that time, she could speak Japanese like a native.

   B: _____

       a. Maybe she can teach me.

       (b.) How did she learn it?

2. **A:** He won't be able to leave the hospital for a long time.

   B: _____

       a. Who's going to take care of him at home?

       b. I'll try to visit him every day.

3. **A:** The whole house is clean.

   B: _____

       a. It's amazing that you were able to do it by yourself.

       b. Who could help you?

4. **A:** We couldn't find a babysitter, so we stayed home.

   B: _____

       a. Well, you made the right decision.

       b. I'm glad that you were able to.

5. **A:** We might go out to dinner tonight.

   B: _____

       a. OK. I was able to meet you there.

       b. Where do you think you'll go?

6. A: Do you know how to swim?

   B: _____

      a. Yes, but not very well.

      b. No, it's too cold today.

7. A: Were you able to go to the meeting last night?

   B: _____

      a. Yes, I could.

      b. Yes, I was.

8. A: What will you be able to do after this English class?

   B: _____

      a. I'll be able to speak English more fluently.

      b. I can speak English more fluently.

F2 Editing

Find the errors in this paragraph and correct them.

My friend Josh might take̶ us to the beach this weekend. The beach isn't far from his house. Josh can to walk there. He is a great swimmer. He could swim when he was three years old! My roommate Nicole doesn't know to swim, so I will probably teach her this weekend. Nicole will able to swim by the end of the summer if she practices every day. May be we'll go sailing this weekend, too. Last Saturday Josh and I was able to go sailing because the weather was great. We could see dolphins near the boat. They were beautiful. Unfortunately, we couldn't touch them. If we're lucky, we can see some dolphins at the beach this weekend.

▶ Beyond the Classroom

Searching for Authentic Examples

Find examples of English grammar in everyday life. Look in an English-language newspaper or magazine, or on the Internet for articles dealing with a famous person's plans for the future. Find five examples of sentences containing modals of future possibility: *may, might,* or *will*. Can you find any examples of *maybe*? Bring your examples to class. How is each example used? Does it show possibility or certainty about a plan? Discuss your findings with your classmates.

Writing

Follow these steps below to write a paragraph about your future after college.

1. Think about the topic. Make notes about what you want to say. Use these questions to help you organize your ideas.
   - What things will you be able to do?
   - What things will you definitely do or not do?
   - What things will you possibly do or not do?

2. Write a first draft. Use modals of future ability and possibility where appropriate.

3. Read your work carefully and circle grammar, spelling, and punctuation errors. Work with a partner to decide how to fix your errors and improve the content.

4. Rewrite your draft.

   After I finish college, I'll probably be able to get a good job. I'll probably look for a job in a bank, but I may not look for a job right away. I could take some more classes at night, but first I might take some time to relax. Maybe I'll go on a vacation. . . .

Modals and Phrases of Request, Permission, Desire, and Preference

How *Not* to Ask for a Raise

A1 **Before You Read**

Discuss these questions.

Have you ever asked for a raise (an increase in pay)? How did you ask? What did your boss say? What are some good ways to ask for a raise?

A2 **Read**

Read this book excerpt to find out about good and bad ways to ask for a raise.

How *Not* to Ask for a Raise

A Case Study

As the manager of her own company, Rachel Franz has been asked for raises by many employees. Sometimes she has agreed and sometimes she
5 hasn't. Franz's decision is often influenced by how an employee asks. Here is a typical request for a raise. Find the mistakes that the employee makes in this situtation.

10   **Robert:** Ms. Franz, <u>could I speak</u> to you for a few minutes?
    Ms. Franz: Can we talk another time? It looks like we have a big problem with
                our computer system and . . .
    Robert: I would rather talk to you now, if possible. It will only take a few minutes.
    Ms. Franz: Well, OK, come in.
15   **Robert:** I don't know if you know this, but I'm getting married next month.
    Ms. Franz: No, I didn't know that, Robert. Congratulations!
    Robert: Thank you. Of course, getting married is quite expensive. Would you
                consider giving me a raise?

Ms. Franz: Well, Robert, your performance review is coming up in six months. I
20   would like to wait until your review.
Robert: But six months is a long time. Could we discuss a raise sooner?
Ms. Franz: We usually don't give raises between reviews, Robert. Now please
          excuse me. I have to find out about this computer problem. Can you
          please ask Kristen to come into my office when you leave?

Analysis

25 Robert made several errors. First of all, it is best to make an appointment with your
boss in advance. Second, try to speak to your boss when things are going well, not
badly. Listen when your boss says that it isn't a good time to talk, and arrange to
speak to him or her later. Third, give your boss a good reason to give you a raise.
Explain that you have more responsibilities at work now, or that you are working
30 longer hours. Show your boss how important you are to the company, not how badly
you need the money. Last, do your homework. Robert didn't know that the company
doesn't give raises between reviews. Robert didn't get a raise, and he has probably
hurt his chances of getting one in the future!

Adapted from *Executive Female*

---

consider: to think about
do your homework: to prepare for something by finding out important information
influence: to have an effect on someone's behavior

performance review: a meeting in which a boss and an employee discuss the employee's work
responsibilities: things that you must do as part of your job

---

A3 **After You Read**

The writer says that Robert made several errors. Check (✓) the four errors that
Robert made, according to the Analysis in the book excerpt.

__✓__ 1. Robert didn't make an appointment with his boss in advance.

_____ 2. Robert didn't speak politely to his boss.

_____ 3. Robert chose a bad time to speak to his boss.

_____ 4. Robert walked into his boss's office without her permission.

_____ 5. Robert didn't have a good reason for his boss to give him a raise.

_____ 6. Robert didn't know the company rules about raises before he spoke to
        his boss.

B Modals of Request; Modals of Permission; *Would Like, Would Prefer,* and *Would Rather*

Examining Form

Look back at the conversation in the book excerpt on page 178 and complete the tasks below. Then discuss your answers and read the Form charts to check them.

1. Find questions with the modals *can, could,* and *would.* (An example is underlined.) What is the subject of each question? What form of the verb follows the subject?

2. Find the expressions *would rather* and *would like.* Which one is followed by the base form of the verb? Which one is followed by an infinitive (*to* + verb)?

MODALS OF REQUEST

Yes/No Questions			
MODAL	SUBJECT	BASE FORM OF VERB	
Can	you	close	the window?
Could			
Will		give	me a raise?
Would			

Short Answers					
YES	SUBJECT	MODAL	NO	SUBJECT	MODAL + NOT
Yes,	I	can.	No,	I	can't.
		will.			won't.

- Modals of request are usually used in questions with *you.*
- We usually use *can* and *will* in affirmative short answers. *Could* and *would* are less common.
- We usually avoid using *won't* in negative short answers because it sounds very impolite and angry.

Affirmative Statements

SUBJECT	MODAL	BASE FORM OF VERB	
You	can / may	borrow	my car.

Negative Statements

SUBJECT	MODAL + *NOT*	BASE FORM OF VERB	
You	cannot / can't / may not	borrow	my car.

Yes/No Questions

MODAL	SUBJECT	BASE FORM OF VERB	
Can / Could / May	I / we	borrow	your car?

Short Answers

YES	SUBJECT	MODAL	NO	SUBJECT	MODAL + *NOT*
Yes,	you	can. / may.	No,	you	can't. / may not.

Information Questions

WH- WORD	MODAL	SUBJECT	BASE FORM OF VERB	
What	can	I	call	you?
When	could	we	make	a reservation?
Where	may	I	put	my coat?

- Modals of permission are most often used in questions with *I* and *we* and in statements with *you*.
- Use *can* and *may* in statements and short answers. Do not use *could*.
- Use *can*, *could*, and *may* in *Yes/No* questions.
- There is no contracted form of *may not*.

(Continued on page 182)

Form • Modals and Phrases of Request, Permission, Desire, and Preference　　181

WOULD LIKE, WOULD PREFER, AND WOULD RATHER

Affirmative Statements

SUBJECT	WOULD RATHER	BASE FORM OF VERB
I	would rather	leave.

SUBJECT	WOULD PREFER/ WOULD LIKE	INFINITIVE OR NOUN PHRASE
I	would prefer	to leave.
	would like	some tea.

Negative Statements

SUBJECT	WOULD RATHER + NOT	BASE FORM OF VERB
I	would rather not	leave.

SUBJECT	WOULD PREFER + NOT	INFINITIVE
I	would prefer not	to leave.

Yes/No Questions

WOULD	SUBJECT	RATHER	BASE FORM OF VERB
Would	you	rather	leave?

WOULD	SUBJECT	PREFER/ LIKE	INFINITIVE or NOUN PHRASE
Would	you	prefer	to leave?
		like	some tea?

Short Answers

YES,	SUBJECT	WOULD		NO,	SUBJECT	WOULD + NOT
Yes,	I	would.		No,	I	wouldn't.

YES,	SUBJECT	WOULD		NO	SUBJECT	WOULD + NOT
Yes,	I	would.		No,	I	wouldn't.

Information Questions

WH- WORD	WOULD	SUBJECT	RATHER	BASE FORM OF VERB
What	would	you	rather	eat?

WH- WORD	WOULD	SUBJECT	PREFER/ LIKE	INFINITIVE
What	would	you	prefer	to eat?
			like	

- *Would rather* is similar to a modal verb. It is followed by the base form of the verb.
- Unlike modals, *would like* and *would prefer* are followed by the infinitive (*to* + verb). They can also be followed by a noun phrase.
- *Would like* is not usually used in negative statements. Use *don't/doesn't want* instead.

  I **don't want** to leave.   I **don't want** tea.
- For contractions with *would*, combine the subject pronoun + *'d*.

B1 Listening for Form

🎧 Listen to these conversations. Write the form of the modals you hear.

1. **A:** Kevin, _____will_____ you start dinner? I'm going shopping.
   ₁

   B: Hmm . . . _____ you get some chocolate ice cream?
   ₂

   A: I _____ buy more ice cream. You know we're both on a diet.
   ₃

2. **A:** _____ I speak with Mrs. Thompson, please?
   ₁

   B: No, I'm sorry. She's in a meeting. _____ you call back in an hour?
   ₂

3. **A:** _____ you _____ a cup of coffee?
   ₁   ₂

   B: No, thanks. I _____ a cup of tea.
   ₃

4. **A:** I _____ to go to the beach with my friends this weekend, but I don't
   ₁

   have any money. _____ I borrow $50?
   ₂

   B: No, you _____. You already owe me $100!
   ₃

B2 Building Questions with Modals

Build eight logical questions. Use a word or phrase from each column.

Can I come with you?

		give	to leave now
can		come	with you
could	I	prefer	me a ride
would	you	like	eat later
		rather	some coffee

Complete these conversations using the words in parentheses. Use contractions where possible. Then practice the conversations with a partner.

1. **Guard:** Excuse me, sir. The sign says <u>visitors may not take</u>
   ₁

   (not/take/may/visitors) pictures inside the museum.

   Visitor: Oh, I'm sorry. I didn't see it. _____
   ₂

   (leave/I/can/where) my camera?

2. **Salesclerk:** _____ (I/help/may) you?
   ₁

   Customer: Yes. I'm looking for a birthday gift for my boyfriend.

   _____ (like/I/get/would/to) him
   ₂

   something special.

3. **Visitor:** _____ (I/park/can) here?
   ₁

   Guard: No, I'm sorry. _____ (can/visitors/park/not) in
   ₂

   this section.

4. **Husband:** _____ (you/will/answer) the phone, please?
   ₁

   My hands are wet.

   Wife: Sorry, _____ (I/not/can). I'm busy. They can
   ₂

   leave a message on the answering machine.

5. **Father:** _____ (you/go/would/like/to) skiing with us this
   ₁

   weekend?

   Daughter: No, thanks. _____ (rather/I/stay/would) home.
   ₂

6. **Waitress:** _____ (order/like/you/would/to) now?
   ₁

   Customer: Yes, I'll have the broiled chicken.

   Waitress: _____ (you/would/prefer) soup or salad as an appetizer?
   ₂

Write the negative form of each sentence. Use contractions where possible. Remember to avoid the negative form of *would like.*

1. I would rather stay home tonight.

   I'd rather not stay home tonight.

2. We would prefer to exercise in the morning.

   _____

3. I would like to call you later.

   _____

4. They would rather live in the suburbs.

   _____

5. He would prefer to buy a new computer.

   _____

6. He would like to finish his work now.

   _____

In your notebook, write short conversations with information questions and answers using these words and phrases. Punctuate your sentences correctly.

1. where/would rather/live/in Hong Kong/in New York City

   A: Where would you rather live, in Hong King or in New York City?
   B: I'd rather live in Hong Kong.

2. who/would prefer/meet/a famous athlete/a famous writer

3. where/would like/eat dinner tonight/at home/in a restaurant

4. what/would rather/do tonight/watch TV/go out

5. how/would rather/ travel/by car/by plane

6. what/would like/buy/a laptop computer/a digital camera

7. what/would rather/eat/cookies/cake

8. where/would prefer/live/in a big city/in a small town

C Modals of Request

Examining Meaning and Use

Read the sentences and answer the questions below. Then discuss your answers and read the Meaning and Use Notes to check them.

- **a.** Will you open the door?
- **b.** Would you open the door, please?
- **c.** Can you open the door, please?

Which request is the most polite? Which request is the least polite?

Meaning and Use Notes

> ### Making Requests
>
> **1A** Use *can, could, will,* and *would* to make requests. *Can* and *will* are less formal than *could* and *would*. We usually use *can* and *will* in informal conversations with friends and family. We use *could* and *would* to make polite requests in formal situations when we speak to strangers or to people in authority.
>
> | Less Formal | More Formal |
> |---|---|
> | *To a Friend:* **Can** you **tell** me the time? | *To a Stranger:* **Could** you **tell** me the time? |
> | *Mother to Child:* **Will** you **be** quiet? | *To a Boss:* **Would** you **look** at my report? |
>
> ---
>
> **1B** Add *please* to a request to make it more polite.
>
> Can you tell me the time, **please**?   Would you **please** look over my report?

> ### Agreeing to and Refusing Requests
>
> **2A** Use *will* and *can* to agree to requests. Do not use *would* or *could*. We generally use *can't* to refuse a request. *Won't* is used for strong refusals, and sounds impolite.
>
> | Agreeing to a Request | Refusing a Request |
> |---|---|
> | A: Will you help me for a minute? | A: **Can** you **help** me decorate for the party? |
> | B: **Yes,** I **will.** | B: Sorry. I **can't** right now. (polite) |
> | A: **Could** you **spell** your name for me? | A: Holly, will you clean up this room? |
> | B: **Yes,** I **can.** It's C-L-A-R-K-E. | B: **No,** I **won't.** (impolite) |

2B Instead of *can* or *will*, we often use expressions such as *OK, sure,* or *certainly* when agreeing to a request.

A: Will you help me for a minute?
B: **OK.**
A: Could you spell your name for me?
B: **Sure.** It's C-L-A-R-K-E.

2C We often say *I'm sorry* and give a reason in order to make our refusal more polite.

A: Can you help me decorate for the party?
B: **I'm sorry,** but I can't right now. **I have a doctor's appointment.**

C1 **Listening for Meaning and Use** ▶ Notes 1A, 1B

A. 🎧 Listen to each conversation. Is the request you hear informal or formal? Check (✓) the correct column.

	INFORMAL	FORMAL
1.	✓	
2.		
3.		
4.		
5.		
6.		

B. 🎧 Listen to the conversations again. Who are the speakers? Look at the choices, and write the correct letter for each conversation. Then discuss your answers with your classmates.

1. __b__   **a.** wife and husband

2. _____   **b.** mother and daughter

3. _____   **c.** two strangers

4. _____   **d.** two friends

5. _____   **e.** student and teacher

6. _____   **f.** employee and boss

A. Choose the best response to complete each telephone conversation.

1.   **Student:** Could you connect me with Professor Hill's office?

   Secretary: _____

   a. No, I won't. He's busy.

   (b.) I'm sorry. He's not in right now. Would you like to leave a message?

2. **Secretary:** Good morning, History Department.

   Student: I'd like to register for History 201. Is it still open?

   Secretary: _____

   a. Yes. Give me your name.

   b. Yes, it is. Could you give me your name, please?

3. **Jenny's friend:** Will you please tell Jenny that I called?

   Jenny's sister: _____

   a. No, I won't. I'm going out.

   b. I won't be here when she gets home, but I'll leave her a note.

4.   **Mark's friend:** Hi. Is Mark there?

   Mark's brother: _____

   a. Sure. Can you hold on a minute?

   b. Certainly. Would you hold, please?

5.   **Client:** Would you please ask Ms. Banes to call me this afternoon?

   Secretary: _____

   a. I'm sorry, but she's out of the office until next week.

   b. Sorry, I can't.

6.   **Student:** Could you send me some information about scholarships?

   Secretary: _____

   a. Certainly.

   b. No, I can't. That's impossible right now.

B. Discuss your answers with a partner. Why did you choose each response? Why was the other response inappropriate?

C. Now practice the conversations with your partner.

C3 Making Formal and Informal Requests

► Notes 1A, 1B

A. Work with a partner. Complete the requests with *can, will, could,* or *would.* (More than one answer is possible for each situation.)

1. **Neighbor A:** _____Can_____ you take in our mail while we're away?

   Neighbor B: I'm sorry, but I can't. I'll be away then, too.

2. **Young Woman:** Excuse me, officer. _____ you please help me?

   Police Officer: Of course. What's the problem?

3. **Parent:** _____ you help me for a minute?

   Child: OK.

4. **Customer:** _____ you put that in a box, please?

   Salesclerk: I'm sorry, ma'am. I don't have any boxes.

5. **Employee:** When you get a chance, _____ you please show me how to use this new computer program?

   Manager: Certainly. How about right now?

B. Work with a different partner. Compare your answers. Be prepared to explain the modals you choose.

C4 Agreeing to and Refusing Requests

► Notes 1–2

Work with a partner. Read each situation. Then take turns making and responding to requests. Use *can, will, could,* or *would* in your requests. Use expressions such as *OK, sure, certainly,* and *I'm sorry* in your responses, and give reasons for refusals.

1. You are at a supermarket. You want the cashier to give you change for a dollar.

   A: Could you give me change for a dollar, please?
   B: Certainly.
   OR
   I'm sorry. The manager doesn't allow us to make change.

2. You are moving to a new apartment. You want your friend to help you move.

3. You would like your friend to lend you $50 until next week.

4. You are on vacation. You want the hotel desk clerk to give you a larger room.

5. You missed class yesterday, and you want your classmate to lend you her notes.

6. You would like your mechanic to repair your car by the end of the week.

D   Modals of Permission

Examining Meaning and Use

Read the sentences and answer the questions below. Then discuss your answers and read the Meaning and Use Notes to check them.

1a. Can I look at your book?   **2a.** May I borrow your book?
1b. Can you speak Russian?   **2b.** Can I borrow your book?

1. Look at 1a and 1b. Which question asks for permission to do something? Which question asks about ability?

2. Look at 2a and 2b. Which question is more formal?

Meaning and Use Notes

> ### Asking for Permission
>
> **1A** Use *can, could,* and *may* to ask for permission. *Can* and *could* are less formal than *may*. We usually use *may* in formal situations when we speak to strangers or to people in authority. You can use *please* to make your request more polite.
>
> *Less Formal*
> *Child to Parent:* **Can I go** outside and play now?
> *Friend to Friend:* **Could I borrow** your pen for a minute?
>
> *More Formal*
> *Business Call:* A: **May I speak** to Ms. Jones, **please**?
>   B: Certainly. **May I ask** who's calling?
>
> ---
>
> **1B** Because *may* is more formal, it is often used in announcements and signs or other printed materials.
>
> *Announcement:* Flight 26 has arrived. Passengers **may proceed** to Gate 2B for boarding.
>
> *Sign:* Visitors **may not park** in numbered spaces.

2A Use *may/may not* or *can/can't* to give or refuse permission. Do not use *could*.

Giving Permission	Refusing Permission
A: Could I hand in my homework tomorrow?	A: Could I hand in my homework tomorrow?
B: **Yes, you may.** Just put it on my desk.	B: **No, you can't.** It's due today.

2B Instead of answering with *can* or *may*, we often use expressions such as *sure, go (right) ahead,* or *certainly* when giving permission.

A: Can I use the computer now?	A: Could I turn on the radio?
B: **Sure.** I'm finished with it.	B: **Go right ahead.**

2C We often say *I'm sorry* and give a reason to make a refusal sound more polite.

A: Could I hand in my homework tomorrow?

B: **I'm sorry,** but you can't. **It's due today.**

D1 **Listening for Meaning and Use** ► Notes 1A, 1B

Listen to these conversations. In each, the first speaker is asking for permission. Who is the second speaker? Look at the choices and write the correct letter for each conversation.

1. __d__   **a.** a boss

2. _____   **b.** a stranger

3. _____   **c.** a mother

4. _____   **d.** a friend

5. _____   **e.** a police officer

6. _____   **f.** a salesclerk

7. _____   **g.** a brother

8. _____   **h.** a teacher

D2 **Asking For Permission** ▶ **Notes 1A**

Look at the pictures. Make sentences to ask permission. Use informal and formal modals as appropriate.

1.

3.

5.

May I look at your map?

2.

4.

6.

D3 **Asking For and Giving or Refusing Permission** ▶ **Notes 1–2**

Work with a partner. Take turns asking for and giving or refusing permission in these situations. Use *can, may,* or *could* in your questions. Use expressions such as *sure, go (right) ahead, certainly,* and *I'm sorry* in your responses.

1. You need to use your classmate's pencil.

   A: *Can I use your pencil for a minute?*
   B: *Sure. Here you are.*

2. You want to rent an apartment. The landlord shows it to you at night. You want to see it again in the daytime.

3. You want to borrow your friend's car this afternoon.

4. You are hungry, and your roommate has some leftover pizza in the refrigerator.

5. You are buying gas. You want to pay by check.

Would Like, Would Prefer, and Would Rather

Examining Meaning and Use

Read the sentences and complete the tasks below. Then discuss your answers and read the Meaning and Use Notes to check them.

1a. I want the check now. **2a.** Do you like ice cream?
1b. I'd like the check, please. **2b.** Would you like ice cream?

1. Compare 1a and 1b. Which sounds more polite?

2. Compare 2a and 2b. Which is an offer? Which asks about likes or dislikes?

Meaning and Use Notes

Stating Desires and Making Requests with *Would Like*

1A *Would like* has the same meaning as *want*. It is often used to talk about desires.

Stating a Desire with Would Like
I'd like to go to China next year. (= I **want** to go to China next year.)

1B *Would like* is also used to make requests. In making requests, *would like* is more polite than *want*. Add *please* to make the request even more polite.

Making a Request with Would Like
I'd like the check, please.   *I want the check. (not polite)

Making Offers with *Would Like*

2 Use *would like* in a question to make a polite offer.

A: **Would** you **like** some coffee?
B: Yes, please. With milk and sugar.

⚠ Be careful not to confuse *would like* and *like.*

Would Like *(to Make an Offer)*	Like *(to Ask About Likes and Dislikes)*
A: **Would** you **like** some coffee?	A: Do you **like** coffee?
B: Yes, please. With milk and sugar.	B: Yes, I do. I drink it every morning.

(Continued on page 194)

3 Use *thank you* to accept and refuse offers. We often give a reason to make our refusal more polite.

Accepting an Offer	*Refusing an Offer*
A: Would you like a seat?	A: Would you like a seat?
B: Yes, **thank you.**	B: No, **thanks.** I'm getting off at the next stop.

4A Use *would like, would prefer,* or *would rather* to ask about and state preferences.

A: **Would** you $\left\{\begin{array}{l}\textbf{like to} \\ \textbf{prefer to} \\ \textbf{rather}\end{array}\right\}$ walk home or take the bus?

B: **I'd like** to walk.

C: **I'd rather** take the bus. It's too far to walk.

4B Use *would rather* with *than* to compare two actions.

I'd rather walk **than** take the bus.

I'd rather play basketball **than** (play) football.

E1 **Listening for Meaning and Use** ▶ Notes 1, 2, 4A, 4B

Listen to each statement. Is the speaker making a request, making an offer, or stating a preference? Check (✓) the correct column.

	REQUEST	OFFER	PREFERENCE
1.	✓		
2.			
3.			
4.			
5.			
6.			
7.			
8.			

Work with a partner. Look at the pictures and take turns making offers, asking about preferences, and responding appropriately. Use *would like, would prefer,* or *would rather.*

1.

A: *Would you like some help?*
B: *Yes, thank you.* OR
   No, thanks. I can carry them myself.

2.

3.

4.

5.

6.

▶ Beyond the Classroom

Searching for Authentic Examples

Find examples of English grammar in everyday life. Watch an English-language television program or movie. Listen for examples of people making requests, asking for permission, expressing their desires, or stating their preferences. Write down three examples and bring them to class. Which examples are more formal and polite? Which are less formal and less polite? Discuss your findings with your classmates.

Speaking

Follow these steps to present a role-play to your class.

1. In pairs, write a dialogue for one of the situations below. Use modals of request, permission, desire, and preference where appropriate.

   - an employee asking for a raise

   - a shy man asking a woman out for a first date

   - a teenager asking parents for permission to have a party

2. Act out the dialogue for your classmates.

> Lee: *Uh, excuse me, Mrs. Smith, could I ask you something?*
> Mrs. Smith: *Yes, Lee. What would you like to discuss?*

Modals and Phrasal Modals of Advice, Necessity, and Prohibition

The Rules

A1 Before You Read

Discuss these questions.

Do you think it is important to get married? Why or why not? How do men and women meet and marry in your culture?

A2 Read

Read the on-line book review about dating on the following page. Would you buy the book?

A3 After You Read

Write *T* for true or *F* for false for each statement.

__T__ **1.** *The Rules* is written for women.

_____ **2.** According to *The Rules*, a woman should call a man on the phone.

_____ **3.** According to *The Rules*, a man should buy a woman a romantic gift for her birthday.

_____ **4.** According to the writer of the book review, women should play games to make men fall in love with them.

_____ **5.** The writer of the book review agrees with the advice in *The Rules*.

BUNDLES OF BOOKS

Book Review

Are these two playing by *The Rules*?

The Rules
Ellen Fein and Sherrie Schneider

An unexpected best-seller, this is a self-help book for women who want to find their ideal man. The basic idea of *The Rules* is that women must play

5 hard to get. For example, *The Rules* states that a woman must not call a man on the phone, ask him to dance, or begin a conversation. She <u>must refuse</u> a date for Saturday if the invitation

10 comes after Wednesday. Further, the authors say that a woman should stop dating a man if he doesn't buy her a romantic gift for special occasions such as Valentine's Day or her birthday.

Ellen Fein and Sherrie Schneider, the authors, say that all women who want to

15 get married have to follow these rules. However, I believe that women should not follow the advice in this book—women who do will end up alone or married to the wrong man.

In my opinion, any woman who follows this advice had better buy a copy of the book for her boyfriend. If she doesn't, how will he know the rules? Women don't

20 have to play games to make men fall in love with them. I believe that a man and a woman ought to know each other very well before they get married. How can two people get to know each other when one of them is following a set of artificial rules?

Reviewed by Janice Harper

---

artificial: not natural

get to know: to spend time with someone and learn about him or her

play games: to behave dishonestly in order to get what you want

play hard to get: to try to attract someone by pretending that you aren't interested in him or her

Valentine's Day: a day (February 14) when people send cards to the people they love

B Modals and Phrasal Modals of Advice, Necessity, and Prohibition

Examining Form

Look back at the review on page 201 and complete the tasks below. Then discuss your answers and read the Form charts to check them.

1. An example of the modal *must* is underlined. Find another example. What form of the verb follows *must*?

2. Find an example of the modal *should*. What form of the verb follows it?

3. Find an example of each of these phrasal modals: *have to, ought to,* and *had better*. What form of the verb follows each of them?

4. Find the negative forms of *must, should,* and *have to*. How is the negative form of *have to* different from the negative forms of *should* and *must*?

MODALS OF ADVICE, NECESSITY, AND PROHIBITION

Affirmative Statements			
SUBJECT	**MODAL**	**BASE FORM OF VERB**	
You	could		
He	might should	buy	a gift.
They	must		

Negative Statements			
SUBJECT	**MODAL + *NOT***	**BASE FORM OF VERB**	
You			
He	should not shouldn't	buy	a gift.
They	must not		

Yes/No Questions			
MODAL	**SUBJECT**	**BASE FORM OF VERB**	
Should	I	buy	a gift?

Short Answers					
YES	**SUBJECT**	**MODAL**	*NO*	**SUBJECT**	**MODAL + *NOT***
Yes,	you	should.	No,	you	shouldn't.

Information Questions				
WH- WORD	**MODAL**	**SUBJECT**	**VERB**	
Where	should	we	go	for dinner?

- *Could, might, should,* and *must* are used to give advice. *Should* and *must* are also used to express necessity. *Must not* is used to express prohibition.
- Like all modals, *could, might, should,* and *must* are followed by the base form of the verb and have the same form for all subjects.
- The contracted form *mustn't* is not usually used in American English.
- Do not use *couldn't* in negative statements of advice.
- *Could, might,* and *must* are not usually used in questions of advice.
- We usually use *have to* (see below) instead of *must* in questions of necessity.

PHRASAL MODALS OF ADVICE AND NECESSITY

Affirmative Statements

SUBJECT	PHRASAL MODAL	BASE FORM OF VERB	
I	have to have got to		
She	has to has got to	call	him.
They	have to have got to		

CONTRACTIONS			
I've	got to	call	him.
She's			

Negative Statements

SUBJECT	DO/DOES + *NOT*	PHRASAL MODAL	BASE FORM OF VERB	
I	do not don't			
She	does not doesn't	have to	call	him.
They	do not don't			

CONTRACTIONS				
I	don't	have to	call	him.
She	doesn't			

Affirmative Statements

SUBJECT	PHRASAL MODAL	BASE FORM OF VERB	
I			
She	ought to had better	call	him.
They			

CONTRACTIONS		
I'd better	call	him.

Negative Statements

SUBJECT	PHRASAL MODAL + *NOT*	BASE FORM OF VERB	
I			
She	had better not	call	him.
They			

CONTRACTIONS		
I'd better not	call	him.

(Continued on page 204)

Yes/No Questions				
DO/DOES	SUBJECT	PHRASAL MODAL	BASE FORM OF VERB	
Do	I			
Does	she	**have to**	**call**	him?
Do	they			

Short Answers					
YES	SUBJECT	*DO/ DOES*	*NO*	SUBJECT	*DO/DOES + NOT*
	you	**do.**		you	**don't.**
Yes,	she	**does.**	**No,**	she	**doesn't.**
	they	**do.**		they	**don't.**

Information Questions				
WH- WORD	*DO/DOES*	SUBJECT	PHRASAL MODAL	BASE FORM OF VERB
Who	**do**	I		
What			**have to**	**pay?**
When	**does**	she		
Why				

- *Have to, have got to, ought to,* and *had better* are used to give advice. *Have to* and *have got to* are also used to express necessity.

- Unlike other phrasal modals, *have to* and *have got to* have different forms for the third-person singular.

- *Had better* looks like a past form, but isn't. It is used to talk about the present and the future.

    You**'d better** call him now.   We**'d better** leave tomorrow.

- In spoken English, we usually use contracted forms of *had better* and *have got to*. The contracted form of *had* for all persons is *'d*. *Have to* does not have a contracted form.

    You**'d better** call him.   You**'ve got to** call him   *You've to call him. (INCORRECT)

- We do not usually use *have got to* or *ought to* in negative statements or in questions.

- We do not usually use *had better* in questions.

🎧 Listen to these sentences. Circle the modal forms you hear.

1. **a.** should
   b. shouldn't

2. **a.** has to
   b. doesn't have to

3. **a.** We'd better
   b. We'd better not

4. **a.** must
   b. must not

5. **a.** have to
   b. don't have to

6. **a.** should
   b. shouldn't

7. **a.** You've got to
   b. You have to

8. **a.** have got to
   b. have to

A. Rewrite these statements as *Yes/No* questions.

1. He should buy a new car. <u>Should he buy a new car?</u>

2. We have to eat at 12. _____

3. They should bring a gift. _____

4. She has to go to class today. _____

5. You have to get a new passport. _____

6. He should see a doctor. _____

B. Write an information question about each underlined word or phrase.

1. <u>Susan</u> should give us the money. <u>Who should give us the money?</u>

2. He has to write <u>a paper for his history class.</u> _____

3. You have to stay in the hospital <u>for two days.</u> _____

4. We should go to the gym <u>on Monday.</u> _____

5. They have to take this form <u>to the Registration Office.</u> _____

6. You should talk to the professor <u>after the class.</u> _____

B3 Writing Contracted Forms

Rewrite these sentences with contractions where possible. If you cannot use a contraction in a sentence, write *No contraction possible.*

1. You had better tell her the truth. <u>You'd better tell her the truth.</u>

2. You have to look for a better job. _____

3. She ought to see a doctor. _____

4. He has got to study more. _____

5. You should not wear jeans to work. _____

6. She has to spend more time with the kids. _____

7. You had better not argue with him. _____

8. You have got to take a trip to the Caribbean! _____

9. He should not waste any more time. _____

10. You do not have to call. _____

B4 Writing Negative Statements

Rewrite these affirmative statements as negative statements. Use contractions where possible.

1. You should ask him to dance. <u>You shouldn't ask him to dance.</u>

2. Jake has to do his homework now. _____

3. Visitors must park here. _____

4. You had better tell your roommate the news. _____

5. Employees have to attend the sales meeting. _____

6. They should buy their son a car this year. _____

7. You must get on that train. _____

8. You should ask for a raise. _____

9. He had better wait until tomorrow. _____

10. You have to be home early. _____

Reduced Forms of *Ought To, Has To, Have To,* and *Have Got To*

I <u>ought to</u> get back to the library.

Yeah, I <u>have to</u> go to class, anyway.

🎧 Look at the cartoon and listen to the conversation. How are the underlined forms in the cartoon different from what you hear?

In informal conversation, *ought to* is often pronounced as /ˈɔt̮ə/, *has to* as /ˈhæstə/, *have to* as /ˈhæftə/, and *have got to* as /hævˈgɑt̮ə/ or /ˈgɑt̮ə/.

STANDARD FORM	WHAT YOU MIGHT HEAR
I **ought to** go.	"I /ˈɔt̮ə/ go."
She **has to** do the work.	"She /ˈhæstə/ do the work."
We **have to** see him now.	"We /ˈhæftə/ see him now."
You**'ve got to** finish today.	"You've /ˈgɑt̮ə/ finish today." OR "You /ˈgɑt̮ə/ finish today."

B5 Understanding Informal Speech

🎧 Matt and Linda are getting married today. Listen to their conversations. Write the standard form of the words you hear.

Conversation 1: At Matt's house

Matt: It's 9:00. We _____ought to_____ leave now.
        ₁

Friend: The wedding is at 10:00. We don't _____ leave until 9:30.
          ₂

Matt: But we _____ be there before the guests arrive.
        ₃

Conversation 2: Later, at the church

Linda: Where's Matt? He _____ come soon! We're getting
          ₁
        married in 15 minutes!

Sister: Maybe I _____ call him at home.
          ₂

Father: Don't worry. He'll be here. We _____ stay calm and wait.
          ₃

Modals and Phrasal Modals of Advice

Examining Meaning and Use

Read these sentences and answer the questions below. Then discuss your answers and read the Meaning and Use Notes to check them.

a. You ought to take that job.
b. You could take that job now, or you could wait awhile.
c. You had better take that job soon, or someone else will.
d. You have to take that job. You need a job!
e. You should take that job.

1. Which two sentences offer advice and have the same meaning?

2. Which sentence expresses the strongest advice?

3. Which sentence makes two suggestions?

4. Which sentence expresses a warning?

Meaning and Use Notes

> **Weak and Strong Advice**
>
> **1** Use *could, might, should (not), ought to, had better (not), have to, have got to,* and *must* to give advice, suggestions, and warnings.
>
> *It's Mary's birthday tomorrow.*
>
> *Weak* • could, might — You **could buy** her flowers.
>
> • should (not), ought to — You **should ask** her what she wants.
>
> • had better (not) — You**'d better buy** something before it's too late.
>
> *Strong* • have to, have got to, must — You **have to buy** her that new book.

Suggestions with *Could* and *Might*

2 Both *could* and *might* are used to make casual suggestions, especially when there is more than one choice.

If you want to get to know him, you **might** invite him for coffee after class, or you **could** call him.

You **could** meet for lunch or dinner.

Advice with *Should* and *Ought To*

3A Use *should (not)* and *ought to* to give advice. *Should (not)* is more common than *ought to.*

You **should get** married in June, when the weather is warm.

You **ought to look** for a new job.

3B You can also use *should (not)* and *ought to* in general statements to express a personal opinion about something.

People **shouldn't** drive when they're tired.

The President **ought to** do more for the environment.

3C Use words such as *I think, maybe,* and *perhaps* to soften your advice or opinion.

<u>I think</u> the President **ought to do** more for the environment.

<u>Maybe</u> you **should get** married in June.

Warnings with *Had Better*

4 *Had better (not)* is stronger than *should (not)* or *ought to.* It is used to give advice with a warning about possible bad consequences. As with *should (not)* or *ought to,* you can use expressions such as *I think, maybe,* and *perhaps* to soften the meaning.

You**'d better study** for the test. If you don't, you'll fail.

You**'d better not make** so many personal phone calls at work, or you'll lose your job.

<u>I think</u> you**'d better see** the doctor, or your cold will get worse.

(Continued on page 210)

> **Strong Advice with *Have To*, *Have Got To*, and *Must***

5A *Have to*, *have got to*, and *must* are used to give strong advice. They often suggest that the situation is serious or urgent.

Your cough sounds terrible. You $\begin{Bmatrix} \textbf{have to} \\ \textbf{'ve got to} \\ \textbf{must} \end{Bmatrix}$ **see** a doctor immediately.

5B Another type of strong advice with *have to*, *have got to*, and *must* is more casual. It shows that the speaker has a strong opinion about something, even though the situation is not serious.

You $\begin{Bmatrix} \textbf{have to} \\ \textbf{'ve got to} \\ \textbf{must} \end{Bmatrix}$ **try** that new restaurant. I ate there yesterday and the food is great!

C1 **Listening for Meaning and Use**　　　　► Notes 1–5

Listen to two people give advice. Who gives stronger advice: Speaker A or Speaker B? Check (✓) the correct column.

	SPEAKER A	SPEAKER B
1.		✓
2.		
3.		
4.		
5.		
6.		
7.		
8.		

Write two suggestions for each question or statement. Use *could* in one suggestion and *might* in the other.

1. Friend: My grades in French are really bad. What should I do?

You: You could study harder.

You might get a tutor to help you.

2. Friend: I need to earn some extra money this summer. How can I find a job?

You: _____

_____

3. Sister: Let's go somewhere special for Mom's birthday. Where could we go?

You: _____

_____

4. Friend: I'm so bored. There's nothing to do around here.

You: _____

_____

C3 **Giving Your Opinion** ► Notes 3A–3C

A. Work with a partner. Take turns asking and answering questions using these words and phrases. Use *should* in your questions. Use *should* or *ought to* in your answers. You can soften your advice with *I think, maybe,* or *perhaps.*

1. men/give women romantic birthday gifts

   A: Should men give women romantic birthday gifts?
   B: Yes, they should. I think men ought to give women romantic gifts all year.

2. women with small children/work

3. men/do housework

4. women/invite men to go out

5. married woman/keep her family name/take her husband's last name

B. Work on your own. Make up two more opinion questions with *should.* Then ask your classmates their opinions.

C4 **Giving Advice** ▶ **Notes 3A, 3C, 5A**

A. Work with a partner. Give two pieces of advice to the person(s) in each situation. Use *you should* in one and *you ought to* in the other. You can soften your advice with *maybe, perhaps,* or *I think.*

1. Sasha has an old car. The car is making a strange noise.

   You ought to buy a new car. Maybe you should fix your car.

2. Today is Monday. Emily has to work today, but she woke up with a sore throat.

   _____

3. Dan isn't doing very well in his math class.

   _____

4. Mr. and Mrs. Chen love their apartment, but it's a little expensive.

   _____

B. The situations have become worse. Give two pieces of strong advice for each situation. Use *you have to, you've got to,* or *you must.*

1. Now Sasha's car has broken down.

   You must not fix this car. You've got to buy a new car.

2. It's Monday night. Emily has a high fever. She feels very sick.

   _____

3. Now Dan is failing math. If he fails, he won't graduate.

   _____

4. The Chens' landlord has increased the rent and they can't afford it.

   _____

C. Work by yourself. Write down three situations of your own. Then ask your partner to give advice.

Look at the pictures and write a warning for each one. Use *had better* or *had better not*.

1. <u>He had better stop the car.</u>   4. _____

2. _____   5. _____

3. _____   6. _____

D Modals of Necessity and Prohibition

Examining Meaning and Use

Read the sentences and answer the questions below. Then discuss your answers and read the Meaning and Use Notes to check them.

1a. Students must show an ID to enter the building.
1b. You have to show an ID to enter the building.

2a. Students must not bring food into the library.
2b. You shouldn't bring food into the library.

1. Which sentence in each pair is formal, and sounds like a rule or a law?

2. Which sentence in each pair sounds more conversational?

Meaning and Use Notes

> **Necessity**
>
> **1A** *Should, ought to, have to, have got to,* and *must* express necessity. *Must* expresses the strongest necessity and is used in formal or more serious situations. We often use *should, ought to, have to,* and *have got to* in conversation to avoid sounding too formal.
>
> Students **should study** their notes before the exam.
> I **have to hurry**. I'm going to be late!
> We**'ve got to send** out the invitations today. The party is next week.
> You **must take** the final exam if you want to pass the course.
>
> ---
>
> **1B** Use *must* to express rules, laws, and requirements, especially in written documents.
>
> Bicyclists **must obey** all traffic lights in the city.
> All couples **must apply** for a marriage license in person.
>
> ---
>
> **1C** *Should, have to,* and *have got to* are often used instead of *must* to talk about rules and laws in less formal English.
>
> The manual says that bicyclists **should obey** all traffic lights in the city.
> I found out that we **have to apply** for a marriage license in person.

Lack of Necessity vs. Prohibition

2 *Don't/doesn't have to* and *must not* have very different meanings. *Don't/doesn't have to* means that something is not necessary—there is a choice of whether to do it or not. *Must not* means that something is prohibited (not allowed). There is no choice involved.

Don't/Doesn't Have To *(Not Necessary)*	Must Not *(Prohibited)*
Your children **don't have to take** these vitamins. If they eat a healthy diet, they'll be fine.	Your children **must not take** these vitamins. They are for adults only.

D1) Listening for Meaning and Use ▶ Notes 1A, 1B, 2

🎧 Listen to these conversations between an employee at the Department of Motor Vehicles and people who call with questions. What does the employee say about each of the topics in the chart? Check (✓) the correct column.

		NECESSARY	NOT NECESSARY	PROHIBITED
1.	take an eye test	✓		
2.	take the eye test at the Department of Motor Vehicles			
3.	need a California license to drive in California			
4.	pay with a credit card			
5.	go to driving school			
6.	drive alone without a learner's permit			

A. Read these public signs. Then explain the signs by completing the statements with *must, don't have to,* or *must not.*

1. SWIMMING POOL FOR APARTMENT RESIDENTS ONLY

   This means that you _____*have to*_____ be a resident of the apartment

   building to swim in the pool.

2. NO PETS ALLOWED

   This means that you _____ bring your pet into the building.

3. CHILDREN UNDER 12 FREE

   This means that children under 12 years old _____ pay

   to go in.

4. NO APPOINTMENT NECESSARY

   This means that you _____ make an appointment.

5. NO EXIT

   This means that you _____ go out this door.

6. ID REQUIRED

   This means that you _____ show identification.

7. HOSPITAL ZONE — NO HORNS

   This means that you _____ blow your car horn in this area.

8. SHIRT AND SHOES, PLEASE

   This means that you _____ wear a shirt to go into this place,

   but you _____ wear a tie.

B. Work with a partner. Discuss the signs in part A. Where do you think you might you find each one?

A. Look at each sign and write a sentence to explain its meaning. Use *must* and *must not*.

1. <u>You must not smoke</u>   3. _____   5. _____

   <u>here.</u>   _____   _____

2. _____   4. _____   6. _____

   _____   _____   _____

B. Work with a partner. What other signs have you seen? Write down the words or draw the images and show them to your classmates. Explain each sign using *have to, have got to,* or *must not.*

You have to turn right.

Work with a partner. Think about your English class. Write sentences about what is necessary, what is not necessary, and what is not allowed. Use *have got to, have to, don't have to, must,* and *must not.*

1. <u>We have to speak English in class.</u>

2. _____

3. _____

4. _____

5. _____

Combining Form, Meaning, and Use

Choose the best answer to complete each conversation. Then discuss your answers in small groups.

1. **A:** Emergency Room. How can I help you?

   B: My daughter fell down the stairs and she's unconscious! Should I bring her in?

   A: _____ wait for an ambulance.
   - **a.** You'd better
   - **b.** You could

2. **A:** Do you like my new dress?

   B: _____ .
   - **a.** Not really. You shouldn't wear that color.
   - **b.** Yes, you don't have to wear that color.

3. **A:** I'd like to pick up my car. Is it ready?

   B: Yes, but you _____ come right away. We're closing in a few minutes.
   - **a.** might
   - **b.** should

4. **A:** I don't have my glasses. What does that sign say?

   B: It says, "Visitors _____ check in at the front desk."
   - **a.** must
   - **b.** ought to

5. **A:** Can we put posters on the wall in our dorm room?

   B: Yes, but you _____ make holes in the walls. It's against the rules.
   - **a.** don't have to
   - **b.** shouldn't

6. **A:** My boss will fire me if I come late again.

   B: _____

      a. Then you'd better be on time from now on.

      b. Then maybe you must not be late.

7. **A:** What do you want for dinner?

   B: I don't care. _____

      a. You should make hot dogs.

      b. We could have spaghetti.

8. **A:** Look at all those people at the exit. We'll never get out.

   B: We _____ use that exit. There's another one in the back.

      a. don't have to

      b. must not

E2 Editing

Find the errors in this paragraph and correct them.

There are many wedding traditions in the United States. One of them is that the
bride ought ^to^ wear "something old, something new, something borrowed, something
blue, and a sixpence in her shoe." The old, new, borrowed, and blue parts are easy
enough. However, a sixpence is an old English coin. It is impossible to find these days,
so most people feel that the bride doesn't has to use a sixpence—any coin will do.
Another tradition is that the groom must not to see the bride before the wedding.
People think that it is bad luck. In addition, many people think that first-time brides
ought wear white and second-time brides could not. However, second and third
marriages are so common these days that many brides feel they must not follow this
rule. One final tradition is that when people get married, they've to save a piece of
their wedding cake for good luck.

▶ Beyond the Classroom

Searching for Authentic Examples

Find examples of English grammar in everyday life. Look in an advice column in a newspaper or magazine or on the Internet for examples of sentences with modals of advice. Bring at least four examples to class. Why is each modal used? Discuss your findings with your classmates.

Writing

Imagine you are the director of a small company. Follow the steps below to write a memo explaining the office rules to new employees.

1. Think about all the things a new employee needs to know. Make notes about what you want to say. Use these categories to help you.

   - office hours
   - lateness
   - appropriate clothing
   - lunch breaks

   - vacation policy
   - sick leave
   - personal phone calls
   - Internet use

2. Write a first draft. Use modals and phrasal modals of advice, necessity, and prohibition.

3. Read your work and circle grammar, spelling, and punctuation errors. Work with a partner to help you decide how to fix your errors and improve the content.

4. Rewrite your draft.

   To: All New Employees
   From: Bob Chang

   Welcome to Architectural Design Solutions. Please read this memo carefully. Before you start work here, you have to . . .

Glossary of Grammar Terms

ability modal *See* **modal of ability**.

action verb A verb that describes a thing that someone or something does. An action verb does not describe a state or condition.

> Sam **rang** the bell.
> I **eat** soup for lunch.
> It **rains** a lot here.

active sentence In active sentences, the agent (the noun that is performing the action) is in subject position and the receiver (the noun that receives or is a result of the action) is in object position. In the following sentence, the subject **Alex** performed the action, and the object **letter** received the action.

> Alex mailed the letter.

adjective A word that describes or modifies the meaning of a noun.

> the **orange** car
> a **strange** noise

adverb A word that describes or modifies the meaning of a verb, another adverb, an adjective, or a sentence. Many adverbs answer such questions as *How? When? Where?* or *How often?* They often end in -**ly**.

> She ran **quickly**.   She ran **very** quickly.
> a **really** hot day   **Maybe** she'll leave.

adverb of degree An adverb that makes adjectives or other adverbs stronger or weaker.

> She is **extremely** busy this week.
> He performed **very** well during the exam.
> He was **somewhat** surprised by her response.

adverb of frequency An adverb that tells how often a situation occurs. Adverbs of frequency range in meaning from *all of the time* to *none of the time*.

> She **always** eats breakfast.
> He **never** eats meat.

adverb of manner An adverb that answers the question *How?* and describes the way someone does something or the way something happens. Adverbs of manner usually end in -**ly**.

> He walked **slowly**.
> It rained **heavily** all night.

adverb of opinion An adverb that expresses an opinion about an entire sentence or idea.

> **Luckily,** we missed the traffic.
> We couldn't find a seat on the train, **unfortunately.**

adverb of possibility An adverb that shows different degrees of how possible we think something is. Adverbs of possibility range in meaning from expressing a high degree of possibility to expressing a low degree of possibility.

> He'll **certainly** pass the test.
> **Maybe** he'll pass the test.
> He **definitely** won't pass the test.

adverb of time An adverb that answers the question *When?* and refers to either a specific time or a more indefinite time.

> Let's leave **tonight** instead of **tomorrow**.
> They've **recently** opened a new store.

adverbial phrase A phrase that functions as an adverb.

> Amy spoke **very softly**.

affirmative statement A sentence that does not have a negative verb.

> Linda went to the movies.

agreement The subject and verb of a clause must agree in number. If the subject is singular, the verb form is also singular. If the subject is plural, the verb form is also plural.

> **He comes** home early.   **They come** home early.

article The words **a, an,** and **the** in English. Articles are used to introduce and identify nouns.

> **a** potato   **an** onion   **the** supermarket

auxiliary verb A verb that is used before main verbs (or other auxiliary verbs) in a sentence. Auxiliary verbs are usually used in questions and negative sentences. **Do, have,** and **be** can act as auxiliary verbs. Modals (**may, can, will,** and so on) are also auxiliary verbs.

> **Do** you have the time?
>
> I **have** never been to Italy.
>
> The car **was** speeding.
>
> I **may** be late.

base form The form of a verb without any verb endings; the infinitive form without *to*. Also called *simple form.*

> sleep   be   stop

clause A group of words that has a subject and a verb. *See also* **dependent clause** and **main clause.**

> If I leave, . . .
>
> The rain stopped.
>
> . . . when he speaks.
>
> . . . that I saw.

common noun A noun that refers to any of a class of people, animals, places, things, or ideas. Common nouns are not capitalized.

> man   cat   city   pencil   grammar

comparative A form of an adjective, adverb, or noun that is used to express differences between two items or situations.

> This book is **heavier than** that one.
>
> He runs **more quickly than** his brother.
>
> A CD costs **more money than** a cassette.

complex sentence A sentence that has a main clause and one or more dependent clauses.

> When the bell rang, we were finishing dinner.

conditional sentence A sentence that expresses a real or unreal situation in the *if* clause, and the (real or unreal) expected result in the main clause.

> If I have time, I will travel to Africa.
>
> If I had time, I would travel to Africa.

consonant A speech sound that is made by partly or completely stopping the air as it comes out of the mouth. For example, with the sounds /p/, /d/, and /g/, the air is completely stopped. With the sounds /s/, /f/, and /l/, the air is partly stopped.

contraction The combination of two words into one by omitting certain letters and replacing them with an apostrophe.

> I will = **I'll**   we are = **we're**   are not = **aren't**

count noun A common noun that can be counted. It usually has both a singular and a plural form.

> orange — oranges
>
> woman — women

definite article The word **the** in English. It is used to identify nouns based on assumptions about what information the speaker and listener share about the noun. The definite article is also used for making general statements about a whole class or group of nouns.

> Please give me **the** key.
>
> **The** scorpion is dangerous.

dependent clause A clause that cannot stand alone as a sentence because it depends on the main clause to complete the meaning of the sentence. Also called *subordinate clause.*

> I'm going home **after he calls.**

determiner A word such as **a, an, the, this, that, these, those, my, some, a few,** and **three** that is used before a noun to limit its meaning in some way.

> **those** videos

direct object A noun or pronoun that refers to a person or thing that is directly affected by the action of a verb.

> John wrote **a letter.**
>
> Please buy **some milk.**

first person One of the three classes of personal pronouns. First person refers to the person (*I*) or people (*we*) who are actually speaking or writing.

future A time that is to come. The future is expressed in English with **will, be going to,** the simple present, or the present continuous. These different forms of the future often have different meanings and uses.

> I **will** help you later.
>
> David **is going to** call later.
>
> The train **leaves** at 6:05 this evening.
>
> I**'m driving** to Toronto tomorrow.

general quantity expression A quantity expression that indicates whether a quantity or an amount is large or small. It does not give an exact amount.

> **a lot of** cookies   **a little** flour
> **a few** people   **some** milk

general statement A generalization about a whole class or group of nouns.

> Whales are mammals.
> A daffodil is a flower that grows from a bulb.

generic noun A noun that refers to a whole class or group of nouns.

> I like **rice.**
> **A bird** can fly.
> **The laser** is an important tool.

gerund An -**ing** form of a verb that is used in place of a noun or pronoun to name an activity or a state.

> **Skiing** is fun.   He doesn't like **being sick.**

***if* clause** A dependent clause that begins with **if** and expresses a real or unreal situation.

> **If I have the time,** I'll paint the kitchen.
> **If I had the time,** I'd paint the kitchen.

imperative A type of sentence, usually without a subject, that tells someone to do something. The verb is in the base form.

> **Open** your books to page 36.
> **Be** ready at eight.

impersonal *you* The use of the pronoun **you** to refer to people in general rather than a particular person or group of people.

> Nowadays **you** can buy anything on the Internet.

indefinite article The words **a** and **an** in English. Indefinite articles introduce a noun as a member of a class of nouns or make generalizations about a whole class or group of nouns.

> Please hand me **a** pencil.
> **An** ocean is **a** large body of water.

independent clause *See* **main clause.**

indirect object A noun or pronoun used after some verbs that refers to the person who receives the direct object of a sentence.

> John wrote a letter to **Mary.**
> Please buy some milk for **us.**

infinitive A verb form that includes **to** + the base form of a verb. An infinitive is used in place of a noun or pronoun to name an activity or situation expressed by a verb.

> Do you like **to swim**?

information question A question that begins with a **wh-** word.

> Where does she live?   Who lives here?

intonation The change in pitch, loudness, syllable length, and rhythm in spoken language.

intransitive verb A verb that cannot be followed by an object.

> We finally **arrived.**

irregular verb A verb that does not form the simple past by adding a -*d* or -*ed* ending.

> put — put — put   buy — bought — bought

main clause A clause that can be used by itself as a sentence. Also called *independent clause.*

> I'm going home.

main verb A verb that can be used alone in a sentence. A main verb can also occur with an auxiliary verb.

> I **ate** lunch at 11:30.
> Kate can't **eat** lunch today.

mental activity verb A verb such as **decide, know,** and **understand** that expresses an opinion, thought, or feeling.

> I don't **know** why she left.

modal The auxiliary verbs **can, could, may, might, must, should, will,** and **would.** They modify the meaning of a main verb by expressing ability, authority, formality, politeness, or various degrees of certainty. Also called *modal auxiliary.*

> You **should** take something for your headache.
> Applicants **must** have a high school diploma.

modal of ability **Can** and **could** are called modals of ability when they express knowledge, skill, opportunity, and capability.

> He **can** speak Arabic and English.
> **Can** you play the piano?
> Yesterday we **couldn't** leave during the storm.
> Seat belts **can** save lives.

modal of necessity **Should** and **must** are called modals of necessity along with the phrasal modals **ought to, have to**, and **have got to**. They express various degrees of necessity in opinions, obligations, rules, laws, and other requirements.

Students **must** take two upper-level courses in order to graduate.

Employees **should** wear identification tags at all times.

We**'ve got to** arrive before the ceremony starts.

modal of possibility **Could, might, may, should, must,** and **will** are called modals of possibility when they express various degrees of certainty ranging from slight possibility to strong certainty.

It **could / might / may / will** rain later.

modal of prohibition **Must not** is called a modal of prohibition when it means that something is not allowed (prohibited).

Drivers **must not** change lanes without signaling.

modal of request **Can, could, will,** and **would** are called modals of request when they are used for asking someone to do something. They express various degrees of politeness and formality.

Can you **pass** the sugar, please?

Would you **tell** me the time?

modify To add to or change the meaning of a word. Adjectives modify nouns (**expensive** cars). Adverbs modify verbs (**very** fast).

negative statement A sentence with a negative verb.

I **didn't see** that movie.

He **isn't** happy.

noncount noun A common noun that cannot be counted. A noncount noun has no plural form and cannot occur with **a, an,** or a number.

information   mathematics   weather

nonseparable Refers to two- or three-word verbs that don't allow a noun or pronoun object to separate the two or three words in the verb phrase. Certain two-word verbs and almost all three-word verbs are nonseparable.

Amy **got off** the bus.

We **cut down on** fat in our diet.

noun A word that typically refers to a person, animal, place, thing, or idea.

Tom   rabbit   store   computer   mathematics

noun clause A dependent clause that can occur in the same place as a noun, pronoun, or noun phrase in a sentence. Noun clauses begin with **wh-** words, **if, whether,** or **that.**

I don't know **where he is.**

I wonder **if he's coming.**

I don't know **whether it's true.**

I think **that it's a lie.**

noun phrase A phrase formed by a noun and its modifiers. A noun phrase can substitute for a noun in a sentence.

She drank **milk.**

She drank **chocolate milk.**

She drank **the milk.**

object A noun, pronoun, or noun phrase that follows a transitive verb or a preposition.

He likes **pizza.**

She likes **him.**

Go with **her.**

Steve threw **the ball.**

particle Words such as **up, out,** and **down** that are linked to certain verbs to form phrasal verbs. Particles look like prepositions but don't express the same meanings.

He got **up** late.

Tom works **out** three times a week.

They turned **down** the offer.

passive sentence Passive sentences emphasize the receiver of an action by changing the usual order of the subject and object in a sentence. In the sentence below, the subject (**The letter**) does not perform the action; it receives the action or is the result of an action. The passive is formed with a form of **be** + the past participle of a transitive verb.

The letter was mailed yesterday.

past continuous A verb form that expresses an action or situation in progress at a specific time in the past. The past continuous is formed with **was** or **were** + verb + **-ing.** Also called *past progressive.*

A: What **were** you **doing** last night at eight o'clock?

B: I **was studying.**

past participle A past verb form that may differ from the simple past form of some irregular verbs. It is used to form the present perfect, for example.

I have never **seen** that movie.

past progressive *See* **past continuous.**

phrasal modal A verb that is not a true modal, but has the same meaning as a modal verb. Examples of phrasal modals are **ought to, have to,** and **have got to.**

phrasal verb A two- or three-word verb such as **turn down** or **run out of.** The meaning of a phrasal verb is usually different from the meanings of its individual words.

She **turned down** the job offer.

Don't **run out of** gas on the freeway.

phrase A group of words that can form a grammatical unit. A phrase can take the form of a noun phrase, verb phrase, adjective phrase, adverbial phrase, or prepositional phrase. This means it can act as a noun, verb, adjective, adverb, or preposition.

The **tall man** left.

Lee **hit the ball.**

The child was **very quiet.**

She spoke **too fast.**

They ran **down the stairs.**

plural The form of a word that refers to more than one person or thing. For example, **cats** and **children** are the plural forms of **cat** and **child.**

possibility modal *See* **modal of possibility.**

preposition A word such as **at, in, on,** or **to,** that links nouns, pronouns, and gerunds to other words.

prepositional phrase A phrase that consists of a preposition followed by a noun or noun phrase.

on Sunday

under the table

present continuous A verb form that indicates that an activity is in progress, temporary, or changing. It is formed with **be** + verb + **-ing.** Also called *present progressive.*

I'm **watering** the garden.

Ruth **is working** for her uncle.

He**'s getting** better.

present perfect A verb form that expresses a connection between the past and the present. It indicates indefinite past time, recent past time, or continuing past time. The present perfect is formed with **have** + the past participle of the main verb.

I**'ve seen** that movie.

The manager **has** just **resigned.**

We**'ve been** here for three hours.

present progressive *See* **present continuous.**

pronoun A word that can replace a noun or noun phrase. **I, you, he, she, it, mine,** and **yours** are some examples of pronouns.

proper noun A noun that is the name of a particular person, animal, place, thing, or idea. Proper nouns begin with capital letters and are usually not preceded by **the.**

Peter   Rover   India   Apollo 13   Buddhism

purpose infinitive An infinitive that expresses the reason or purpose for doing something.

In order to operate this machine, press the green button.

quantity expression A word or words that occur before a noun to express a quantity or amount of that noun.

a lot of rain   **few** books   **four** trucks

real conditional sentence A sentence that expresses a real or possible situation in the **if** clause and the expected result in the main clause. It has an **if** clause in the simple present, and the **will** future in the main clause.

If I get a raise, I won't look for a new job.

regular verb A verb that forms the simple past by adding -ed, -d, or changing **y** to **i** and then adding -**ed** to the simple form.

hunt — hunted

love — loved

cry — cried

rejoinder A short response used in conversation.

A: I like sushi.

B: **So do I.**

C: **Me too.**

response An answer to a question, or a reply to other types of spoken or written language. *See also* **rejoinder**.

> A: Are you hungry?
> B: Yes, **I am**. Let's eat.

> A: I'm tired of this long winter.
> B: **So am I.**

second person One of the three classes of personal pronouns. Second person refers to the person (**you**, singular) or people (**you**, plural) who are the listeners or readers.

separable Refers to certain two-word verbs that allow a noun or pronoun object to separate the two words in the verb phrase.

> She **gave** her job **up**.

short answer An answer to a **Yes/No** question that has **yes** or **no** plus the subject and an auxiliary verb.

> A: Do you speak Chinese?
> B: **Yes, I do. / No, I don't.**

simple past A verb form that expresses actions and situations that were completed at a definite time in the past.

> Carol **ate** lunch.
> She **was** hungry.

simple present A verb form that expresses general statements, especially about habitual or repeated activities and permanent situations.

> Every morning I **catch** the 8:00 bus.
> The earth **is** round.

singular The form of a word that refers to only one person or thing. For example, **cat** and **child** are the singular forms of **cats** and **children**.

stative verb A type of verb that is not usually used in the continuous form because it expresses a condition or state that is not changing. **Know, love, resemble, see,** and **smell** are some examples.

subject A noun, pronoun, or noun phrase that precedes the verb phrase in a sentence. The subject is closely related to the verb as the doer or experiencer of the action or state, or closely related

to the noun that is being described in a sentence with *be*.

> **Erica** kicked the ball.
> **He** feels dizzy.
> **The park** is huge.

subordinate clause *See* **dependent clause**.

superlative A form of an adjective, adverb, or noun that is used to rank an item or situation first or last in a group of three or more.

> This perfume has **the strongest** scent.
> He speaks **the fastest** of all.
> That machine makes **the most noise** of the three.

tag question A type of question that is added to the end of a statement in order to express doubt, surprise, and certainty. Certain rising or falling intonation patterns accompany these different meanings.

> You're feeling sick, **aren't you**?
> He didn't leave, **did he**?

tense The form of a verb that shows past, present, and future time.

> He **lives** in New York now.
> He **lived** in Washington two years ago.
> He**'ll live** in Toronto next year.

third person One of the three classes of personal pronouns. Third person refers to some person (**he, she**), thing (**it**), or people or things (**they**) other than the speaker/writer or listener/reader.

three-word verb A phrasal verb such as **break up with, cut down on,** and **look out for.** The meaning of a three-word verb is usually different from the individual meanings of the three words.

time clause A dependent clause that begins with a word such as **while, when, before,** or **after.** It expresses the relationship in time between two different events in the same sentence.

> **Before Sandy left,** she fixed the copy machine.

time expression A phrase that functions as an adverb of time.

> She graduated **three years ago.**
> I'll see them **the day after tomorrow.**

transitive verb A verb that is followed by an object.

> I **read** the book.

two-word verb A phrasal verb such as **blow up, cross out,** and **hand in.** The meaning of a two-word verb is usually different from the individual meanings of the two words.

used to A special past tense verb. It expresses habitual past situations that no longer exist.

> We **used to** go skiing a lot. Now we go snowboarding.

verb A word that refers to an action or a state.

> Gina **closed** the window.
> Tim **loves** classical music.

verb phrase A phrase that has a main verb and any objects, adverbs, or dependent clauses that complete the meaning of the verb in the sentence.

> Who **called you**?
> He **walked slowly.**
> I **know what his name is.**

voiced Refers to speech sounds that are made by vibrating the vocal cords. Examples of voiced sounds are /b/, /d/, and /g/.

> **b**at   **d**ot   **g**et

voiceless Refers to speech sounds that are made without vibrating the vocal cords. Examples of voiceless sounds are /p/, /t/, and /f/.

> u**p**   i**t**   i**f**

vowel A speech sound that is made with the lips and teeth open. The air from the lungs is not blocked at all. For example, the sounds /a/, /o/, and /i/ are vowels.

wh- **word** Who, whom, what, where, when, why, how, and **which** are **wh-** words. They are used to ask questions and to connect clauses.

Yes/No **question** A question that can be answered with the words **yes** or **no.**

> Can you drive a car?   Does he live here?

Index

This Index is for the full and split editions. Entries for Volume A are in bold.